DIY, Dammit!

JOSELYN HUGHES

DIY, Dammit!

A Practical Guide to
CURSE-FREE Crafting

HarperOne
An Imprint of HarperCollins Publishers

HarperOne

HarperCollins books may be purchased for educational, business, or sales promotional use. For information please e-mail the Special Markets Department at SPsales@harpercollins.com.

HarperCollins website: http://www.harpercollins.com

HarperCollins®, 🏭®, and HarperOne™ are trademarks of HarperCollins Publishers.

FIRST EDITION

Designed by Ralph Fowler

All photographs by Melly Lee Photography, www.mellylee.com, except photograph on page 141, courtesy of Mamrie Hart

Library of Congress Cataloging-in-Publication Data
Hughes, Joselyn.
    DIY, dammit! : a practical guide to curse-free crafting / Joselyn Hughes. — First edition.
    pages   cm
  ISBN 978-0-06-237146-1
  1. Handicraft.   I. Title.
  TT145.H84   2015
  745.5—dc23   2015009854

15 16 17 18 19   SCP   10 9 8 7 6 5 4 3 2 1

To my handy and funny
mom and dad

CONTENTS

Decorate

Gift

Wear

Entertain

Organize

Introduction

I t all began a couple of years ago. I went home for Christmas and my lovely sister-in-law offered me a delicious apple cider caramel. As I housed one after another, after another—and yikes, almost all of them—I slipped into a blissful, fantastical, sugary stupor. In my dreamlike state, **I vaguely remember asking her where in the hell she purchased such sugary delights.** "I made them," I *think* she said, as I drifted off into a diabetic coma. When I woke up and became somewhat coherent, I asked her again. "I made them," she replied. "Super easy. I'll e-mail you the recipe."

And so it began. I came home to L.A., ready to makes some caramels and change lives. Off to the grocery store I went. Candy thermometer? Check. Apple cider? Check. Recipe? Check. "Super easy," I repeated, clicking through photos on the DIY website. I couldn't wait to sink my teeth into those cavity creators. It was go time.

Well.

Fast-forward to a few days later in my kitchen. I'm exhausted, frazzled, and questioning the meaning of life. Apple cider caramels, more like apple cider TERRIBLES. I didn't understand what wasn't working. The recipe only had five steps and I followed them *to a tee*. Once, twice, three times a failure. (Maybe four or seven, if we're being honest.)

I couldn't get the caramels right. Eventually, I gave up.

I still don't know what went wrong. And that's okay. At least that's what my therapist tells me.

And while I was upset, I had to laugh at myself for having such high hopes and turning into such a frantic psycho when I wasn't able to do it myself.

Bottom line: This stuff wasn't as easy as I'd thought. The directions said it was easy, the pictures implied it was easy, but there wasn't *one thing* easy about it. I'd rather have had the directions explicitly tell me it was possible to lose your mind while trying to make them than tell me it was so simple. **Who were these sadistic liars who made these devil candies look so, well, sweet?**

So I started thinking . . . Why do people feel that showing their missteps, their disasters, their breakdowns is such a *bad* thing? Especially when it's so entertaining?

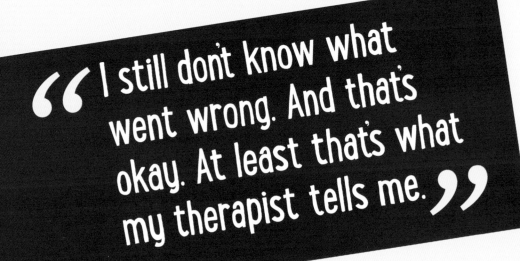

“I still don't know what went wrong. And that's okay. At least that's what my therapist tells me.”

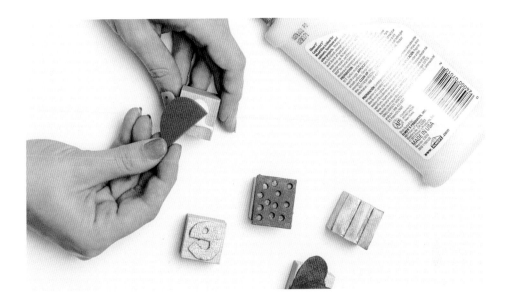

Newsflash: It's the whole Internet. Everyone's striving to be the most perfect version of themselves: furiously untagging themselves in unflattering posts, writing manifestos about how they're oh so politically correct, and posting endless pictures of their weddings, including the classic black-and-white "I'm a very serious bride staring out a window, and even though I look so somber, I'm far happier than you have ever been" profile picture. You know what I'm talking about. It's an image thing. Even *Beyoncé* has been accused of Photoshopping Instagram pics before posting them. "The Bey?! BUT I THOUGHT YOU WOKE UP LIKE THAT!"

Internet perfection does nothing for DIY. It actually makes it harder. I want you to love crafting, and that's not going to happen with the way things are currently going in the DIY world. Those three-step crafts never turn out the way they're supposed to. That reclaimed wood centerpiece did *not* wake up like that. DIY is far from perfect, and it's much more fun when you accept the imperfection and do it (yourself) anyway.

DIY, Dammit! is about being honest and forgiving of your failure instead of chaining it to a pole under your basement stairs like some hideous horror movie creature that murders every HVAC technician who comes to call. Who wants to keep yelling "DON'T GO DOWN THERE!!!" every ten minutes anyway? Not me. I have a water heater that needs fixing.

As such, this book is not a typical approach to doing it yourself. It's *my* approach, which is WAY better. I'm not Martha Stewart. Not even close. And sorry, Marth, but I don't want to be you—though a criminal record would give me a lot more street cred.

Truth is, I love to craft, and I suck at it. But that doesn't stop me. I've adopted the motto "If at first you don't succeed, then DIY again." And now my weakness can be your strength. Because I already made the mistakes—so you don't have to!

> " I'm not Martha Stewart. Not even close. And sorry, Marth, but I don't want to be you. "

How This Book Works

This is *not* a self-help book. But I am helping you help yourself. Let's just call it a help book.

First, give yourself a break from any judgment, criticism, or negative thoughts you may be feeding yourself when it comes to DIY. **This book contains everything you need to have a blast while you craft:** it's a guide, an instructor, a life coach, a comedian, an animal lover, and a friend. Come to think of it, this is all you really need in *life*. Hold this book close to you. Don't ever let it go.

Practically speaking, there are crafts. Lots of them. All tested, attempted, and cursed at by me. There are also many crafts that are *not* in here, because I did them and they simply are not worth it. I have the scars to prove it. Most of them emotional, but if you look very closely, you can see a battle wound I acquired on my hand from cutting an avocado once. While that technically doesn't have anything to do with crafting, it was a lesson. And a damn fine one. These are the things I've saved you from. What you have here are the good ones, the crafts that won't make you cry and scream "WHYYYYYY?" like Nancy Kerrigan in 1994.

There are ideas for decorating, organizing, and entertaining. Crafts to wear, crafts to gift. There are affordable, easy-to-find supply lists for each project; simple directions you can follow, even with a strong beer buzz going; and recommendations on how you can make your DIY experience more fun and effective than mine was. If you're feeling lazy, look for the ones that rank low on my super scientific scale of "Dammits" (that's a 1 or a 2 on a scale from 1 to 5). These are the ones that even I was able to nail on the first try. If you're feeling ambitious, there are also a couple of real showstoppers that'll make you realize you are capable of great things—very great things indeed.

So let's roll up our sleeves—or put on a tank top—and DIY, dammit!

Why DIY?

When I used to hear the term "DIY," I would imagine Martha Stewart wearing a tool belt loaded with essential crafting tools, with one hand on her hip and the other holding a glue gun high above her head in triumph. She'd be standing on a mountain of perfectly made crafts, grinning from ear to ear, proud of her massive and ever developing creation. Her hair would, of course, be perfect. When is her hair not perfect?

Now when I hear "DIY," I see *me,* wearing an outfit covered in glue, paint, and glitter, with one hand holding my half-completed craft together and the other holding a camera, filming it. I'm not standing on so much of a mountain as I am a very, very messy array of various craft supplies, most of which I haven't even used in my project. **My hair, of course, is pretty messed up, and one of my dogs most likely just farted, so I'm making a sour face.** But I too am grinning, very proud of my creation. Especially if it was completed without me having a mental breakdown.

I'm the first to acknowledge that the reality of DIY is a lot less glamorous than the Internet, magazines, and television would have us believe. But that doesn't mean it's unattainable.

Anyone can DIY, and that includes you.

The whole do-it-yourself thing covers a lot of territory, but in this book, we're going to focus on the artsy-adorable-fun kind instead of the rip-out-and-renovate-your-bathroom kind. As much as I'd love to take a sledgehammer to my crappy vanity, I would have no idea how to handle broken porcelain and it would most likely make my landlord super pissed. So crafting it is.

We also will not be focusing on the outdated or downright cringe-worthy crafting of previous decades. Long gone are the days when crafting was all papier-mâché and crocheted trivets. **DIY crafting has become a wildly hip thing to do, and everyone's getting in on it.** I guess that's what happens when the economy takes a dive and you don't get a job after college. Take THAT, my arts, entertainment, and media management degree!

Whether you're broke, unem-ployed, or just plain bored, my mom always told me, if you want some thing done, do it yourself. She also said corned beef comes from cows that eat corn, so she's not right about

everything, but she means well. And she may not have been referring to craft projects when she would tell me to do it myself, but she makes a great point. You can't depend on other people to do things. You have to take action.

In a world of convenience and endless choices, it's pretty easy to sit back and have other people make things for you. Which means it's even more powerful when you produce something all on your own. **You're deciding to create something from nothing.** Like this book, for example. No one else is going to write it for me, so here I am, writing it.

I'm proud of that. And when you make something, you should be proud of yourself too.

You made that. Do you know how badass that is? Let it sink in: you're crafty! And while having DIY swag does put you in a different category than most, wildly boasting about your accomplishment isn't the only reason to DIY. There are quite a few other benefits to the crafting game that are much more noble than bragging rights.

Benefits of DIY Crafting

By choosing DIY, you are wisely choosing to:

→ SAVE MONEY

I am not the most frugal person, but when I see a seventy-dollar price tag on a pillowcase, my wallet weeps. When you DIY, you can make a pillowcase in under thirty minutes for under five bucks (see page 35). It's completely doable! I want you to see the DIY light and follow it. And when you do, you're going to save a ton of ca$h. Mo' money, mo' problems. Less money, you're probably DIYing.

→ REUSE THINGS

This planet has plenty of stuff on it already. Why not look at old things in a new way and give them new uses? Think outside the box, and then turn that box into something more useful (see page 229). When you do this, you're spreading the knowledge that a sweater can absolutely, in fact, become three other things if you want it to. Which can inspire others to think outside the box. See? Even thinking is reusable.

→ FEED THE CREATIVITY BEAST WITHIN

You might not think it, but all of us are innately artistic in some way. We have a little tiny creativity beast that lives inside us. Don't think I don't know about that dried pasta necklace you made in kindergarten. It was gorgeous and I don't understand why your mother didn't wear it more often. Our creativity beast doesn't have any power if we don't feed it. Try giving the little guy a crumb and see what happens. I have a hunch it's gonna feel great.

Our creativity beast doesn't have any power if we don't feed it.

→ BOSS AROUND A CAN OF PAINT

You are your own boss when you craft. You make up the rules, and if one of them involves yelling at a can of paint, you can make that happen. You can even craft a to-do board to boss yourself around on if you feel like it (see page 221). Your boss at the office would *never* allow that. DIY puts the control in your hands. Personally, I need to have power over *something* in my goddamn life—even if that control's over Popsicle sticks and fabric glue. So give it a shot! That's not an order; it's a suggestion. I am not your superior, just a fellow crafter. We're all equals here at DIY, Dammit.

→ MELLOW OUT

Crafting is relaxing. I know when I'm engaged in a creative activity, I kind of zone out in a very peaceful way. It's like yoga for your brain, man. Stitch your way into Zen. Or a very calming sleep mask (see page 171). And don't forget about feeling proud of yourself for taking the initiative to DIY. Good vibrations are everywhere when you're creating. Bask in that serotonin, baby.

→ MAKE SOMETHING YOU CAN'T FIND AT A STORE

Journey knew what they were talking about when they wrote "Any Way You Want It." When you DIY, you are producing a one-of-a-kind original. That is dope as shit. DIY allows you to make something exactly the way you want, when you want. Become a DIY rock star on your own terms. Uniqueness is something to celebrate, so rock out and don't stop believin'.

When you DIY, you are producing a one-of-a-kind original. That is dope as shit.

Pry yourself away from your laptop and do more than just reblog funny Tumblr posts all day.

→ **GET AWAY FROM THE SCREENS**

It's the Fault in Our Phones. They're our constant entertainment, companion, and communication devices. But you can pry yourself away from your laptop and do more than just reblog funny Tumblr posts all day. Instead, make something tangible. Like a case for your device (see page 245). I promise it's possible. And THEN you can post all about it online (using the hashtag #DIYDammit, of course).

→ **LEARN A NEW SKILL**

I still haven't mastered wood burning, but every once in a while I break that wood burner out and practice. Same goes for using gold leaf, spray painting, crocheting, and essentially every single crafting skill that exists. I'm no pro and probably won't ever be one. But I have learned a lot by trying. It helps me figure out how to do other new things. And even cooler still, I can teach my friends what I've learned so they can try it out. You'll want to share the love too when you add to your bag of crafting tricks and techniques (see page ALL OF THEM).

I think the most basic reason for crafting and creating is that there is an inherent satisfaction that comes with doing it yourself. **You're making something real out of an idea in space and using your own handiwork to bring it to life**. You'll have an attachment to your project, an ownership that you wouldn't have otherwise.

The best part of all of this is *it's easier than you think*. And nothing is better than things that are easy. Nothing! Take it from a lazy person: me. Of course, once you have the easy stuff down and you feel comfortable, you can keep challenging yourself with more difficult things. Only if you want to—no pressure. But I promise it's worth it.

Because let's be honest: if crafting was too hard, I wouldn't be writing this book.

" Because let's be honest: if crafting was too hard, I wouldn't be writing this book. "

Why Dammit?

Making mistakes is human. Embracing them is hilarious. Watching someone fail is entertaining because we all get it. Millions of people try to do a myriad of things every day. The operative word being "try." Despite what you've been told your whole life, just because you try doesn't mean you succeed. Sorry, the truth hurts. So do scissors, X-ACTO knives, wire, sisal rope, splinters, superglue, and a bunch of other dangerous elements that you expose yourself to while crafting. The struggle is real. Craftin' ain't easy.

You know when you fall flat on your face in front of a crowd? There's a moment right before you get up when you can choose to feel embarrassed or choose to brush it off, smile, and say something funny, like "Who put that banana there?" or "I've fallen and I can't get up!" or "Global warming isn't real!"

Crafting has caused me more pain and suffering than you could imagine, but that hasn't stopped me from doing it. I'm still pretty bad at most things I try for the first few times, so I've accepted that I'm going to fall down. A lot. And you might too. Give yourself a break! No one is perfect (except star quarterback of the Green Bay Packers, Aaron Rodgers).

What I'm trying to say is that failure is everywhere. It's kind of

> ## "It's NOT normal to be able to craft without messing up, starting over, and swearing a lot. "

beautiful. We've all heard the story of how Michael Jordan was cut from his high school debate team. And glee club. And he farted once in physics and everyone laughed at him. So then he took up basketball and was cut from that team as well. What a loser, right?! Well, legend has it he turned out okay. But I don't believe in legends; I believe in you.

So buck up, kiddo. It's NOT normal to be able to craft without messing up, starting over, and swearing a lot. Just because there are cute li'l pics on the Internet, that doesn't mean crafting's going to be easy for you. Though now that you've bought this book it should be *somewhat* less complicated. I hope.

The moral of the story is if you can take failure lightly and keep your eyes on the prize, you'll go far. There's no need to beat yourself up when something goes wrong. Just shake it off and try again until you achieve your ideal outcome. **If you're still struggling, try to let yourself laugh.** If that means logging on to YouTube and watching an episode of *DIY, Dammit!*, I fully support that. Chuckle at my mistakes!

And speaking of mistakes, I'm well aware that there are plenty of potential problems with doing it yourself, such as having poor time management, being clumsy, having a grouchy roommate who won't let you use the kitchen table for DIYing, not having access to the right tools and supplies, not being able to follow directions or listen to authority, lacking confidence, being hungover, and feeling as though you'll always be in the shadow of Martha Stewart.

Sure, that was a lot of reasons. Don't let a few *buts* stop you from trying though. JLo has a huge butt and she's shaken that thing straight to the top.

Still doubtful? Let's talk it out.

YOU: BUT I DON'T KNOW HOW.

Me: Then it's a good thing you have this book in your hands. At one point in your life you didn't know how to do *anything* and were pooping in your pants on the reg. Look at you now! You're doing great. Keep reading.

YOU: BUT I DON'T HAVE TIME FOR THIS.

Me: I get it. We're all "busy." But part of the reason you're so busy is you're running around telling everyone how busy you are. Try carving out a time to make things. To experience things. To practice some patience. To not just be concerned with being busy and to engage yourself in activities that benefit the greater good: you.

YOU: BUT IT'S GONNA LOOK LIKE SHIT.

Me: Um, I wouldn't do that to you. Homemade-looking crafts are for toddlers and people with no taste. Cool people have taste; that's why you bought this book. I don't like things to look terrible, so I have done my best to only include crafts in this book that will end up looking pretty cute with minimal effort. That being said, it's extremely difficult to get things right on the first try. Or the second. And that's okay. Breathe.

YOU: BUT BUYING IT IS EASIER.

Me: Dude. There's a reason human beings made a shift from making everything ourselves to programming metal robots to do it all. It's easier, more convenient, and more cost effective. But that robot doesn't have a heart. That robot's lacking thoughtfulness. That robot's just that: a robot. Everything's going to be the same when it comes from a robot. You can make an original, personal creation that no one's ever seen or will see again, and that's rad. Beat that, heartless robot.

YOU: BUT I DON'T HAVE ORIGINAL IDEAS.

Me: Me neither! You don't have to reinvent the crafting wheel. This is about trying something out, seeing what comes of it, and maybe, just maybe, your own ideas will start flowing one day. But don't worry about those right now. Worry about me. It's been forty-five minutes since I ordered a large pepperoni and sausage, and the Pizza Tracker is not even loading. I might not make it.

YOU: I FEEL SO MUCH BETTER NOW! BRING ON THE CRAFTS!

Me: Slow down there, old friend. I'm still dropping knowledge.

As I was saying, this book is a great way to try out some projects without judging yourself, getting frustrated, or throwing everything into the trash and burning it. It usually takes me a few attempts to get the result I'm looking for. There are some areas of crafting and life that I'm just not particularly good at, and that is totally okay. I don't always have to be great at everything or friends with everyone or the life of the party. I *do* always have to triple-check whether or not my straightening iron is turned off. But that's just my OCD.

So here we are. I'm here for you, we're in this together, and you can do this.

Yikes, so serious. Go ahead and insert a fart joke here.

Three things you *don't* need to worry about when it comes to crafting:

1. *Having a designated space.* I'll craft anywhere. I usually end up in the middle of the floor wherever a TV is nearby so I can watch my *Dance Moms*, play with my dogs, and craft.
2. *Having skills in anything.* This is what Google is for.
3. *What people think.* Unless you're making this in front of a crowd, and in that case it would be hard for anyone to ignore the constant judgment of the public, but you're not, so knock it off.

Three ways to help you focus and not be distracted:

1. Try *working for twenty-five minutes* or longer chunks, with small five-minute breaks in between so as not to overindulge in work OR play OR staring at timers.
2. Pick out a prize to *reward yourself* with upon completion of your goal. (Mine's always eating five pounds of FroYo while listening to Katy Perry's greatest hits.)
3. *Install blocking software* or apps on your computer/tablet/phone so you don't end up in a Tumblr/Twitter/Vine spiral. (I should do that, since I checked those sites fifty-five times while constructing this sentence.)

Three random tips that I'm grouping together because I already started this groups-of-three thing:

1. *Wear shitty clothes* while crafting so you don't ruin your nice ones.
2. *Practice safety first:* goggles make you look like a dork in science class, but you'll be happy it's not an eye patch after that staple gun goes awry.
3. *Be nice to yourself.*

QUIZ: What Kind of Crafter Are You?

It's the question you've been waiting for.

Wait, did you know that question was coming and were you waiting for it? If so, you might want to drop this book and head over to a psychic school, you incredible visionary.

Back to the subject: a quiz that will determine your true crafting personality. Don't be scared, okay? **This is ALL fun; I promise. The most fun. So let's get jiggly with it, shall we?**

1. **What do you typically make when you DIY?**
   a. Everything. Why wouldn't I?
   b. Whatever's trending online.
   c. Depends on my mood!
   d. I'm not sure *what* you'd call it . . .

2. **When you're looking for inspiration, where do you look?**
   a. A bustling farmers' market, a summer's breeze, the morning dew.
   b. Runways: fashion, airport, or otherwise.
   c. The Internet, obviously.
   d. Everywhere!

3. **When you get frustrated with your DIY, what do you do?**

   a. I. DON'T. GET. FRUSTRATED.

   b. Throw it out and move on to the next, cooler one.

   c. Smash it, regret it, then immediately start over.

   d. Start it on fire, then dance like no one's watching.

4. **If you were stranded on an island, what one DIY supply would you bring?**

   a. I probably wouldn't get stranded on an island, because I'd make a DIY raft ASAP and get the hell out of there.

   b. Spray paint in the latest color.

   c. Superglue! (Fixes every-thing.)

   d. Not sure what it's called, but it's, like, in a bottle.

5. **Which of the following guides you the most when you craft?**

   a. My brain.

   b. My sense of style.

   c. Jelly beans, sometimes. Dumplings, always.

   d. My previous life's soul. (I was a fisherman in Egypt.)

6. **What is rickrack?**

   a. What *isn't* rickrack?

   b. Stuff from the '70s.

   c. I think it's trim?

   d. A rapper.

7. **Why do you craft?**

   a. CRAFTING IS LIFE.

   b. It's super-dupes trendy.

   c. I like to make things!

   d. I get to express myself.

8. **How do you react when you are injured while crafting?**

   a. I don't. No pain, no gain.

   b. I take a picture of it and post it online to see how many sympathy likes I get.

   c. Band-Aids and love.

   d. Is it a physical injury or an emotional one?

9. **What would your Etsy shop be called if you had one?**

   a. I wouldn't. Etsy's for amateurs.

   b. CHICCRAFTZ.

   c. DIYDammit, duh.

   d. The Etsy-Betsy Spider.

10. **What do you think when you enter a craft store?**

    a. This layout is *all wrong*.

    b. Why are there so many old people here?

    c. OMG, WHAT AM I GONNA MAKE?!

    d. Oooo, a candy aisle!

11. **A crafting session usually lasts . . .**

    a. AS LONG AS IT F'ING TAKES.

    b. As long as it takes to document it online.

    c. As long as it takes to finish it, even if that means a cupcake break (or seven).

    d. Time is merely a concept that humans developed to oppress one another and themselves.

12. **Are you on Pinterest?**

    a. Pinterest is for amateurs.

    b. Duh.

    c. Of course!

    d. Is Pinterest a dating site? If so, I'm down.

13. **How much space do you allot to craft supplies in your home?**

    a. Put it this way: instead of a man cave, I have a craft cave.

    b. Eh, not much. I clear out outdated supplies as often as possible.

    c. Not enough.

    d. I share my space with everything around me equally.

14. **What word best describes you as a crafter?**

    a. Precise.

    b. Artistic.

    c. Laid-back.

    d. Pickles.

Results

You did it! Now tally up your answers and find out what kind of crafter you are below!

✓ **If you answered mostly A, you are a Martha Stewart, a Crafting Savant.**
You're a perfectionist and genius crafter who has to make everything yourself to maintain your power. No one sees your mistakes because you've never let them. You're a boss, but you're also terrifying. Why not make the beer poncho (see page 185)? While you're at it, slug a few of those brewskis back and relax a little.

" You're not too high-strung and can laugh at your mistakes. Basically, you're perfect. "

If you answered mostly B, you are a Taylor Swift, a Crafting Trendsetter.

You always know what's in style and you take risks in your crafting. Sometimes weird risks, but your bravery is admirable. You're bold, exciting, and—naturally—all about social media. But you probably need to take off the stilettos, put your phone down, and craft like a real person. Try making Mirror Fun (see page 209), snapping some selfies, hashtagging them #DIYDammit, and making that ish go viral!

If you answered mostly C, you're a ME, a Crafting Cool Person!!!

Holy crap—this is so exciting. Never imagined I'd find myself by taking a quiz in a crafting book! You're the right blend of crafter—you know when to forge ahead and when to quit. You're not too high-strung and can laugh at your mistakes. Basically, you're perfect. You should make the Platter with Panache (see page 199). You'll get to use all kinds of techniques, have the patience to finish the project, and get to reward yourself with an adorable gift!

If you answered mostly D, you are a Miley Cyrus, a Crafting Space Cadet.

The Tasmanian devil of the craft world, you don't have time to follow directions, to wait for glue to dry, or to finish your project. That means you usually end up with a mess of craft supplies . . . and a mess of a project. While I admire your free spirit and your never-ending well of creativity, you might have a hard time getting it together. Start by tackling the Cute-as-a-Cupcake Garland (see page 205) and move up from there. Plus, you can hang it up after you craft and have your own personal party! We all win.

Decorate

I try not to judge people.

It's wrong and unfair and a terrible way to go about being a human ... unless you've seen where they live.

A person's house tells you absolutely *everything* you need to know about who they are. Do they have shag carpeting? Are they way into clowns? Do they leave pubes all over their bathroom floor? Do they hoard cats? Did something just drip on you? Should you run out of their house and into a more public area because by the looks of their living room they are *definitely* a serial killer?

Personal space is just that: PERSONAL. And decorating that space is the purest form of self-expression available. It's what we did before lying about ourselves on social media.

In days of yore, you could browse someone's bookshelves, sift through record albums ("sifting" has been replaced by "scrolling"), and see all the places that person had been and how intimidated by them you should or shouldn't be.

Again, I am in no place to judge, but leave me alone in your apartment and I will know what led to your recent breakup and just how seriously you take food expiration dates.

I also expect my own space to reflect "me," whether aspirational or otherwise. Thus, if you were to step foot in my home (which means you've passed my

two very well-trained guard dogs—impressive) you could see that I've created a bright, fun space that makes me happy. How? I took charge and DIYed that shit. I decided what I wanted and where I wanted it. I didn't wait for someone else to make it and sell it to me. I've got DIYed artwork, candles, pillows—you name it. I even orchestrated what I see every morning when I wake up: "FUCK THIS" (see Puff Banner on page 51).

I love that sign and it means a lot to me. It is a perfect combination of my love of cuteness and my philosophy in life. Just fuck this and do what YOU want, not what's trendy or in a catalogue or what you think people on TV would think is cool. Stop trying to talk to them, by the way. They can't hear you.

This is all to say that your decor is essentially *you,* and the best way to make sure it's speaking the truth is to take control and make it yourself. **These crafts here give you a starting point. Make them your own, make them say what you want them to say.** Which very well might be "FUCK THIS."

I heart easy crafts!

Nailed It!

Difficulty rating:

Not all of us are "natural" artists. Take this three-year-old I used to babysit, for example. He couldn't stay within the lines, let alone identify which color autumnal leaves are supposed to be. I told him to quit art and take up something he was better at, like throwing animal crackers on the floor and laughing at his own farts. You're welcome, three-year-old. I just saved you a very painful attempt at an art career.

Point is, art isn't easy.

But you know what is? Hammering nails.

This DIY is here to prove that you too are an artist, even if you can't stay inside the lines. It's a lot of bang for your buck, so let's **hammer** this home and show the world you're as tough as **nails.** Knock on **wood,** this one should be easy.

29

MATERIALS

- paint (optional)
- wood plaque or piece of wood with at least one flat surface
- template (available at DIYDammit.com, or draw one of your own)
- scissors
- tape
- hammer
- ⅝-inch finishing nails
- yarn, string, or embroidery floss (in the color of your choice)
- glue

1. If you want to paint your wood piece or plaque, do that first and let it dry.

2. Print out or draw a template on a piece of paper—an object, word, shape, etc.—and cut it out, like Joey Gladstone.

3. Center your template on the wood (you can tape it down if you want).

4. Hammer the nails around your shape, spacing them about ¼ inch away from one another, until you've outlined the whole shape.

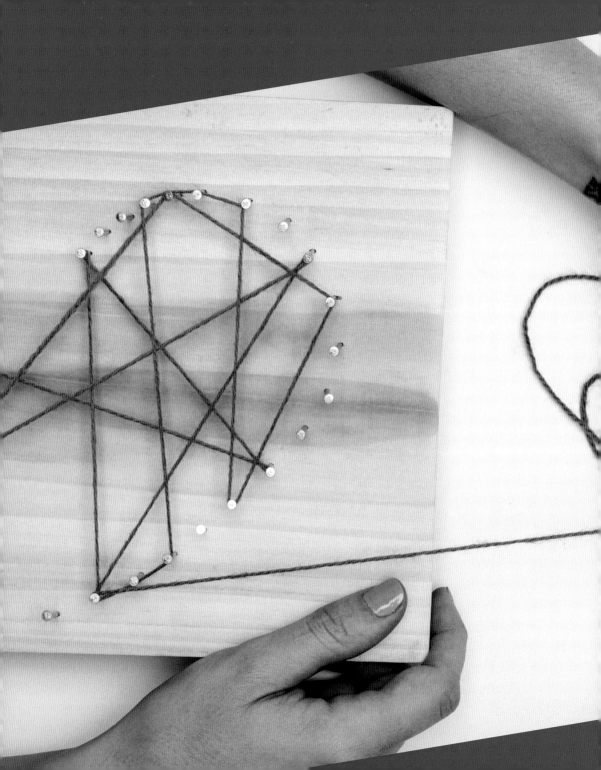

5. Remove the template.

←----------- **6.** Tie the yarn, string, or embroidery floss around one nail (you can glue the end down if you like) and begin to wrap it around the remaining nails as you see fit. (I like to go around the outline at least a couple of times so it stands out.) This does not have to be perfect by any means.

7. When you feel you've adequately strung your nails, tie off the end and glue that end down.

SQUEEZE
ME

Ah...comfortable
crafty cushions
of cuteness.

Cutie Pie Pillows

Difficulty rating:
(unless you go easy on
the embellishments)

only have pillow talk with my pillows. Why? Because their sole purpose is to make me comfortable and I love them for that. Why? Because I love being comfortable. Why? Because I'm not a robot. Why? Because my human parents created me with human genes and didn't build me out of metal robot parts.

I love pillows so much I just started making them. Why? Because, surprisingly, pillows are one of the most simple crafts out there. Why? Few supplies, basic structure, minimal effort. Plus, with a few modifications, you can morph your pillows into exactly what you want to match your decor. So this is one of those crafts that you absolutely need to do instead of spending forty bucks on some fancy schmancy pillow in a store.

Let's make some pillows.

Why not?

MATERIALS

- fabric (wash the fabric before you cut it, so it can preshrink if it's going to)
- cloth measuring tape
- fabric scissors (these are special and fancy and worth buying FYI)
- fusible interfacing (optional)

- iron
- glass-head pins (plastic heads will melt under the iron!)
- sewing machine
- decorations: puffs, lettering, felt, ribbon, etc.
- pillow

You're making a basic envelope pillowcase. No zippers = no hassle. This chart will tell you how much fabric you'll need based on the size of your pillow.

Pillow size	Front piece (cut one)	Back pieces (cut two)	Total approximate yards (of a standard 45-inch-wide bolt)
12" × 12"	12½" square	9" × 12½"	½ yard
14" × 14"	14½" square	10" × 14½"	½ yard
16" × 16"	16½" square	11" × 16½"	½ yard
18" × 18"	18½" square	12" × 18½"	¾ yard
20" × 20"	20½" square	14" × 20½"	1 yard
27" × 27"	27½" square	17" × 27½"	1¼ yard
12" × 16"	12½" × 16½"	11" × 12½"	½ yard
14" × 28"	14½" × 28½"	14½" × 18"	1 yard

1. Cut your pieces of fabric. The two back pieces are going to overlap and create your envelope. If you're going to add interfacing, cut out three pieces of the same sizes as your three fabric pieces. (Even though it's an extra step, I recommend using interfacing. This stuff makes the fabric more durable and is easy to apply—you just iron it on.)

2. Fold and iron down ¼ inch on one of the long sides of each back piece to encase the raw edge of the fabric.

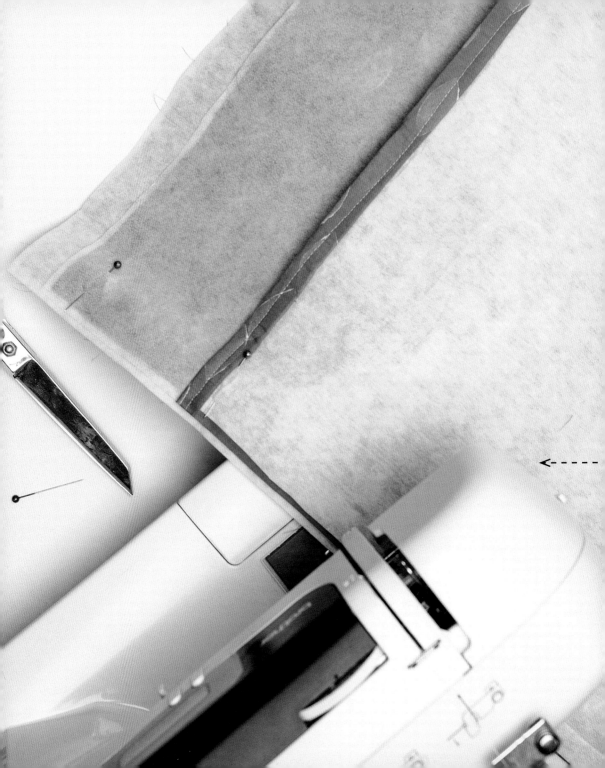

3. Pin the ¼-inch edges down so they're ready to be sewn.

4. Sew the beasts! (Say this like "Kill the beast" from *Beauty and the Beast* and it'll make you smile mid-craft. You're welcome.)

5. Place the fabric for the pillow front right side up. And place the two back pieces right side down on top of the front, with their long stitched edges in the middle. This results in the two back pieces overlapping—that's okay. You want the sides of the fabric that will be on the outside of the pillow to be on the inside at this point.

6. Pin around the edges of the fabric to hold all three pieces together.

7. Again, using a ¼-inch seam allowance, sew around the edges of the pillowcase. (Seam allowance is the area between the edge and the stitching line on any two pieces of material being stitched together.)

8. Once you're done, cut the pillowcase corners at a 45-degree angle (this makes the corners end up more pointy and more corner-y).

9. Flip the pillowcase right side out!! Then stuff it with the pillow insert. You did it!

Feel free to add embellishments, like I did. For the pom-poms, I first made them, then sewed them into the corners of the pillow. You can also use fabric glue to glue on felt pieces or other embellishments (the softer, the better) or iron on letters to convey a message.

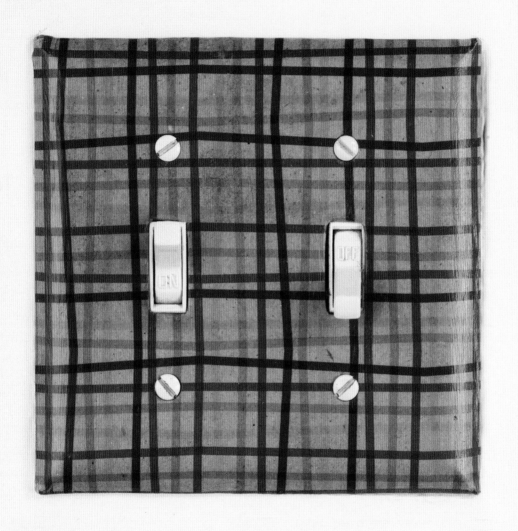

And just like that, a crafty switcheroo in no time.

Do the Light Thing

Can you imagine a life where you're super boring? Maybe you can; I don't know your life. But you shouldn't want to. You shouldn't want anything to be boring.

Which brings me to switch plates. They silently, tirelessly allow you to fondle them day in and day out while making you feel great because, technically, you're financially stable if the lights still work. Meanwhile, they're sentenced to a lifetime of beige boringness.

Thank them by jazzing them up with a cute print, wrapping paper, or even washi tape. This is one of those DIYs that anyone can easily do, including *moi,* and that's saying a lot.

Let's extreme-makeover these switch plates and show 'em what they've been missing. Turn OFF boring and turn ON your DIY skills. And brighten your day in more ways than one.

MATERIALS

- switch plate (use your existing one)
- fabric or paper (covering a plate with washi tape is another fun option—just apply and brush it with a coat of Mod Podge)
- scissors and/or X-ACTO knife
- foam brush
- Mod Podge

1. Lay your switch plate on your fabric or paper and trace around it, adding a half-inch or so overlap on each side.

2. Cut this shape out.

3. Using your foam brush, apply a coat of Mod Podge to the front of your switch plate.

4. Lay the fabric or paper over the switch plate, smoothing it down around all the edges. You'll have to use your scissors or an X-ACTO knife to cut a slit at a 45-degree angle at each corner so the material can fully adhere to the switch plate when it's folded over onto the back.

5. Apply Mod Podge to the back edges of your switch plate, and wrap the material around the edges onto the back. Trim any excess.

6. Cut an X in the holes where the light switches will come through the plate (when it's remounted). Wrap the fabric or paper to the back side and Mod Podge it down. You can poke holes in the screw holes with your scissors or X-ACTO knife as well.

7. Coat the entire switch plate in a layer of Mod Podge to create a nice finish.

8. Let it dry, then remount it.

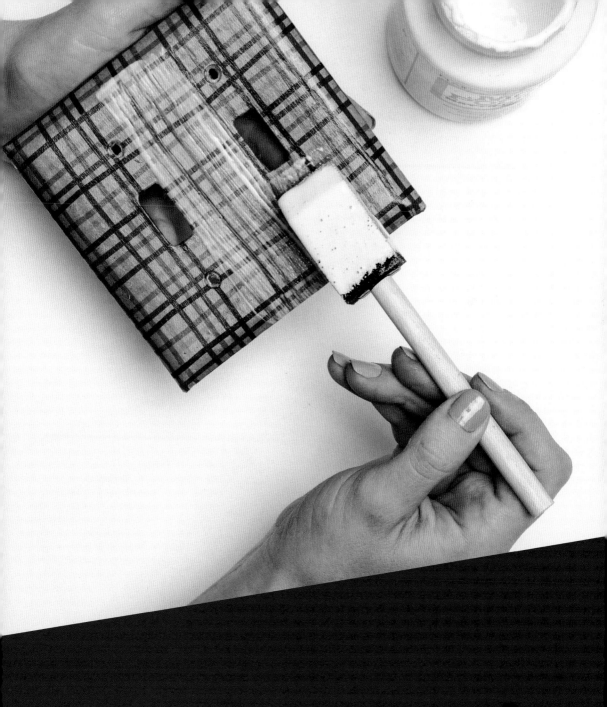

Sharpie Mirror Art

Difficulty rating: ⚒⚒⚒⚒

I think it was Thomas Edison who said genius is 1 percent inspiration and something yadda yadda about perspiration. Which, as I interpret it, means he was probably a sweaty guy. Ew.

But that whole thing about genius being part inspiration is real. Inspiration is wonderful, so why not slip that 1 percent in where you can?

This DIY is a nice way to remind yourself to "smile" or "love" or whatever mushy inspirational self-help phrase makes you take a minute to remind yourself to be happy.

This is a feel-good DIY, and you should feel good. You're reusing, you're recycling, and you're making something you can check yourself out in, in case there's something stuck in your teeth.

Everyone wins.

MATERIALS

- old picture frame
- Krylon Looking Glass Mirror-Like spray paint
- Sharpie paint markers
- spray paint for the frame (optional)

1. Take the glass out of the picture frame.

2. Spray the glass with Looking Glass spray paint, about five coats. Let it dry completely between each coat.

3. When it's fully dry, flip the glass over and outline your design, word, object, etc., with the paint markers and decorate the glass as you'd like. Let it dry.

4. If you want to paint the frame as well, do so and let it dry too.

5. Put the glass back into the frame and display it!

Puff Banner

Saying something offensive in a nice way is really satisfying. Go ahead. Try it now. Maybe say "You fucking suck." But gently, as if you were talking to a tiny baby bunny lying on a bed of daisies.

See?

I don't want to puff this craft up too much, but as far as I'm concerned, it's easily the cutest, softest way out there to make a statement. And the statement doesn't have to be offensive. It can be anything you want. After all, it's covered in puffs! You can get away with anything!

It's just so puffin' cute. Is there a word containing "puff" that isn't?

Not a puffin' one.

MATERIALS

- paper
- X-ACTO knife or scissors
- cardboard
- washi tape
- hot glue gun with hot glue sticks

- pom-poms
- pronged frame picture hangers (1–2 per letter)
- baker's twine

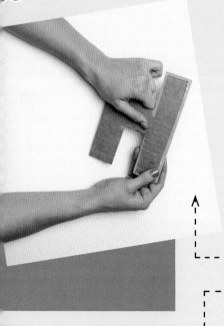

1. On paper, print out your word(s) in a large, easy-to-read typeface. Cut out and trace each letter onto cardboard.

2. Cut the letters out of the cardboard.

 3. Line the edges of the cardboard letters with washi tape (makes it look nicer).

 4. Hot-glue the pom-poms to the cardboard letters. (Have fun with this. There's no rhyme or reason to it, unless you want there to be.)

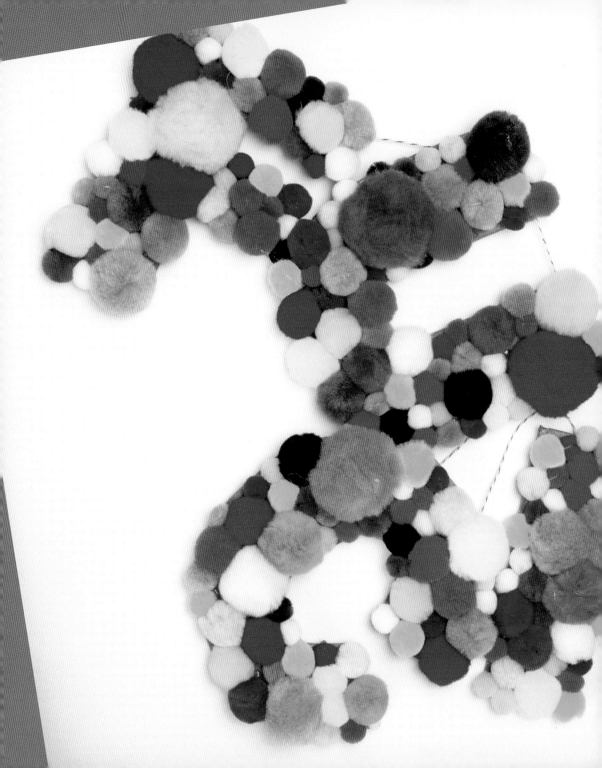

5. Add picture hangers to the back of each letter and hot-glue them for extra support. (Some letters will require more than one hanger.)

6. String each hanger with baker's twine and hang the letters up.

This doormat
ain't no chump.

Timber! Doormat

Difficulty rating: 🔨🔨🔨🔨

Doormats, historically, have garnered a terrible rep. They're walked over, scuffed upon, and left out in the cold. Literally. But that doesn't mean they have to look like shit.

Your doormat should look like it's read *Eat, Pray, Love*. Your doormat should look like it's been skinny-dipping with boys and ran with the bulls in Spain. But most important, your doormat should say "Step on me and remember who you've stepped on, because I'm adorable and hard to forget. I am doormat, hear me roar."

So let's make the cutest goddamn doormat you've ever seen and take back the word "doormat" for us real doormats out there. Wait, I'm not a doormat. **Don't be a doormat!** Make one.

MATERIALS

- ruler or measuring tape
- ¾ × 1½ × 24-inch wood boards (I found these at Home Depot in the precut wood section; probably get at least eight boards, but it depends on how large you want to make your mat)
- power drill with a ⅜-inch drill bit
- wood stain and finish or paint
- ¼-inch nylon rope

1. With a ruler or measuring tape, measure out on the narrower side of each piece of wood where your holes will be, and mark each with an X. They can be close together or farther apart, but measure each piece of wood the same. (I made four holes on each board and evenly spaced them out.)

2. Using the power drill, drill through the Xs. (Be safe! Have someone else do this if you're unfamiliar with drills and whatnot.)

3. Stain and finish or paint the boards and let them dry. (I used a natural finish on mine, but different color paint combinations or stain combinations could be very cute.)

4. Cut a length of the rope that's about one and a half times the width of what you're planning your doormat to be (based on the quantity of boards you plan to use).

5. Knot one end of the rope. Stick the other end through one set of holes in the boards, knotting the rope in between each board to keep them secure. When you've gone through all the boards, finish the rope off with a knot and trim it. Then repeat the same with each set of holes, cutting and knotting, until you have a completed mat.

Snugglicious Pet Bed

Difficulty rating: (or 379/5 if you're a dog)

P ets will sleep just about anywhere. They don't need a special bed. They don't even know what a bed is. But as owners, we need to give them beds because we need to prove to ourselves that we're great caretakers. So great that we could probably take care of an actual human child one day. *Probably*.

Kids are much harder, because of all the talking and caretaking and passing along values and whatnot, but with pets, a nice bed pretty much qualifies you as a great parent. Look what I made for you! You're my hairy little baby! Love me! Stop licking your butt!

Since most of the furry friends I have are happy to sleep on any surface whatsoever, I think it's a safe bet that yours too will appreciate you transforming your favorite sweatshirt (or one you were about to throw away) into a bed. Again, pets don't know the difference between your favorite and about-to-throw-away sweatshirts. And if they do, run. They know too much and will tell everyone what you do when you're alone.

MATERIALS

- sweatshirt (size depends on the size of your pet)
- sewing machine
- measuring tape
- sewing chalk
- sewing pins
- stuffing material such as fiberfill (or possibly an old pillow)

1. Turn the sweatshirt inside out.

2. Sew the edges of the collar together.

3. Mark a line from armpit to armpit across the chest or back of the sweatshirt with the measuring tape and sewing chalk.

4. Pin the sweatshirt along that line and sew. (You can also hand stitch this.)

5. Pin the edges of the sleeves to the edges of the sweatshirt, from the armpit down to the hips, and sew them together. (Also can be hand stitched.)

6. Fill the sleeves with stuffing, plus fill the center/chest area of the sweatshirt or stuff it with an old pillow. (STUFF EVERY PART ONLY AS FULL AS YOU WANT IT TO BE.)

7. Fold under the cuffs of each sleeve and sew them shut.

8. Pin and sew the bottom edge of the sweatshirt shut.

9. Decorate the bed accordingly, remembering that dogs are color blind.

A Note About Dogs and Crafting

Although I encourage my dogs to participate and be a part of every project I take on, dogs are not helpful at all with crafting. They walk through paint and track it all over your house. They chew on yarn and most felts. They're scared of glue smells. But I have to say, I've learned a lot from my dogs. Like, don't give up. The cat next door is a bitch. Pee on the things you want before someone else does. Love everyone, and be the best friend you can. Also, life is awesome. Enjoy it. Bark, bark.

Light
that
sucker
up!

Tin You-Can-Do-It Candle

Difficulty rating: 🔨🔨🔨

Tin cans are great containers, but they look like junk. I don't want a buncha junk sitting around my house; it's no good. So we're making them spiffy and turning them into candles. No worries, earth. We got you.

And once you start making candles yourself, you'll never go back to those overpriced ones that have names like Cinnamon Breeze or Melon Melody Madness. You can give them your own names instead.

May I suggest naming one after me? For example, Jazzy Jos has a nice ring to it. And if you make me a candle, you can totally call me Jos.

Jos saying.

MATERIALS

- tin can
- spray paint (optional)
- Sharpie paint markers
- hot glue gun with hot glue sticks
- soy wax wick
- skewer or stick
- soy wax chips
- scent (optional)
- color (optional)
- scissors

1. Clean your tin can. You can also spray paint it with a base color if you desire, and let it dry.

 2. Paint a design onto the can with paint markers.

3. Hot-glue the wick into the bottom of the can—make sure you've purchased the right size (based on the diameter of the tin can).

4. Wrap the top of the wick around the skewer or stick, and place the skewer or stick across the top of your can, so when you pour the wax, the wick stays in place and centered (so it will burn evenly).

5. Melt the wax chips according to the package directions, adding scent and color if that's your jam (it's worth it).

6. Pour the wax into the can and let it harden completely.

7. Trim the wick to ¼ inch and light.

Permanent Planter

Difficulty rating: ⚒ ⚒ ⚒

Terra cotta? More like terra notta.

That was a great joke. I wrote it when I was in high school pottery class. And by pottery class, I mean ditching school to sit in a Burger King parking lot with a bunch of cute skater boys, as rebellious sophomores often do.

I was shopping for cute planters recently and couldn't find any options outside of plain old terra cotta. We get it: earthenware and planting go hand in hand, blah, blah, blah.

How about we try something different, like this simple concrete planter? You don't need a hard hat to make this happen, just a few supplies and some DIY magic. Oh, and some patience. My first few attempts at this failed. But that's my fault for not waiting long enough for the concrete to harden, not the concrete's fault. So I get overexcited about planters! Can you blame me!?

MATERIALS

- 2 plastic storage containers, one slightly larger than the other—see the instructions. (Any fun bowls or molds are welcome here too. Don't be afraid to try some different things.)

- nonstick cooking spray

- gloves

- pourable concrete mix (like QUIKRETE FastSet)

- paint (optional)

- plant

- potting soil

1. Make sure the smaller plastic container can fit inside the larger container, leaving enough room for a substantial amount of concrete—I'd say about ½ inch on all sides.

2. Spray both containers with nonstick cooking spray: the inside of the larger one, the outside and bottom of the smaller one.

3. Put your gloves on and mix up your concrete according to the directions on the package. You can do this inside the larger plastic container, or do it in another container and then transfer it to the larger plastic container. Whatever floats your boat.

Press the smaller container into the wet concrete inside the larger plastic container, making sure it's evenly spaced and the concrete is evenly distributed. (If you'd like, you can create a small cylindrical shape and put this in the middle of the bottom of the larger container so that the final planter will have a hole for drainage. I'm not patient, so I did not do this.)

5. Let the concrete dry for at least 24 hours. I did NOT leave mine to dry long enough, and wouldn't you know it, disaster struck.

6. Squeeze and pull your plastic containers apart to unearth your new concrete planter. (Hopefully yours doesn't fall apart. I definitely had to try a couple of times to get it right.)

7. If you like, paint the outside of the container, and let it dry.

8. Plant a plant in it!

Whoops!

Navigating a Craft

From Idea to Store to Finished Project

Ah, so you've picked out a cute project. Congrats. You have a good eye, and on top of that, you've decided to get crafty. It's a bold choice but a good one. You've taken the first step.

The problem with transitioning from "I can make that" to "I should make that" to "I'm going to make that" to "HOLY SHIT I MADE THAT!" is that it doesn't always happen. We make promises to ourselves, to each other. Like how some guys say they'll put the toilet seat down, or they'll call you right back, or they'll remain faithful, and then they cheat on you with a beautiful, intelligent costar. Wait, whoops! That's something else. Too late—it's already written down, KYLE. I'm kidding. His name was Brad. William Bradley Pitt. Google him if you have to, but know it was a while back and our breakup was *nasty*. (I miss you, B.)

What I mean to say is that just because you've SAID you're going to DIY that doesn't mean you do. So when you decide to take that idea and bring it to fruition, you have just become pregnant with a DIYD idea. **A tiny little spool of thread that will only be sewn if you head to the craft supply store and make it happen.**

You can make that craft real. You hold that power! Which is why you shouldn't waste it and tease the world with false promises and half-made projects. It's not fair to us *or* them.

Okay, I'll get down off my soapbox now. It's kind of high up and slippery, since it's made out of soap. Just keep the DIYD hope alive, and you'll make it to . . .

The next step, which is gathering your DIY supplies. There are several routes here. Now, I generally don't recommend going to a brick-and-mortar store, since the Internet offers wares vaster than one could possibly fit into a strip mall, but depending on how strong your craft urges are—how much you need that DIY—you may need to pull up a cart and do some serious damage in a Michaels.

Just know that a craft supply store is a place where the one thing you need is always magically missing from the shelves. You might get lost. You might get confused. You might feel overwhelmed, surrounded by hardcore crafters who mean serious business. You're going to have to wait in a line behind an old lady who pays for her knitting needles with pennies. It's its own special kind of shopping experience.

So again, Internet. But do what you need to.

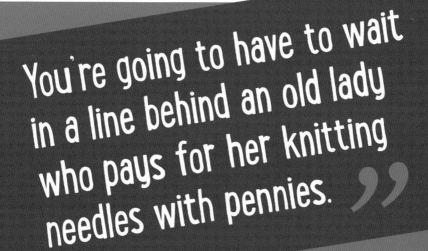

" You're going to have to wait in a line behind an old lady who pays for her knitting needles with pennies. "

Internet

Pros: You don't have to leave the house, it's usually cheaper than a store, a lot of variety is available, and you can check Tumblr any time you need to during the buying process.

Cons: You can't make sure it's exactly what you need, the supplies take a couple of days or weeks to arrive, you have to pay for shipping, and you can check Tumblr the whole time you're purchasing the supplies, extending the purchasing time by four to five hours.

Store

Pros: It's closer than Amazon's warehouse, you can physically see the products, you can ask questions about the supplies, and you don't have to get onto the information superhighway to get there.

Cons: You have to leave the house, you have to wait in line, it's potentially out of stock of something you want, and someone might judge the sweatpants you've been wearing for three days.

I've broken down the most common kinds of craft supplies and what you can expect from them. **After you read this, it's on you.**

The DIYD Guide to Craft Supplies

Glue: The ooey-gooey substance that holds things together. It's very easy to use too much because it's hard to know exactly how strong/messy/sticky it is and whoops your project is ruined because instead of paying attention to it, you're reading this. Should've thought faster.

Glitter: The clinger on-er and parasitic disease of the craft world, mysteriously able to find its way EVERYWHERE, no matter how careful or clean you think you're being. Don't be fooled by its razzly-dazzly, shiny nature. It's a trick.

Paintbrushes: Tools used to distribute paint evenly on a surface that seem very innocent yet are completely okay with destroying your wrists as you use them. They will always act like they can do the job until you're halfway through with

it and realize you should've used a bigger brush/paint roller/airbrush instead.

Hot glue gun: A seemingly nonthreatening gun-type apparatus that heats up a hard stick of glue and turns it into steaming hot, soft, 800-degree lava, with a temperamental trigger that will always manage to squeeze out just enough glue to burn the fuck out of your hand.

Scissors (aka skissors): Stab sticks that if not sharp enough will ruin your craft. If they are too sharp, they will also probably ruin your craft, plus rip apart the skin around your thumb while doing so.

Printer: A machine able to produce images of your choosing to craft with—that is, of course, if it hasn't run out of paper/toner/ink/self-confidence and decided to pout like a teenager and refuse to install on your laptop.

Sewing machine: A mechanical monster for which, before operating, you're required to weave thread through what could only be called a teeny tiny metal boot camp obstacle course from hell. If you succeed in loading the thread, you have only the grace of God to guide you from there. Just try not to sew your own hand.

Measuring tape or ruler: A math-related tool, so already it's troublesome. Either a stick or ribbon with scores and numbers on it that should help you figure out things unless you're too impatient to use it or hate math like a regular person (me).

Iron: Another very hot tool that has the power to burn your face off, especially on a steam setting. Ironing fabric is a really helpful way of showing how crookedly you cut it, and why are you so bad at cutting fabric?

Hammer and nails: Two vital pieces of information about these tools

are (1) hammers hate your thumbs and (2) nails hate walls. Keep that in mind the next time you decide to hang a picture. Seems sooooo easy. It's not.

X-ACTO knife: A sharp mini dagger used for fine cuts and punctures in crafting but also, realistically, a pretty badass weapon. You're packing when you've got one of these in your craft den. I'm sorry, did you think I was just a helpless little crafter? *Wha-BAM!* THINK AGAIN.

Mod Podge: Mod Podge is the Miss Congeniality of the craft supply world. It's kind of like glue but more of a liquid that you should probably paint onto everything you make because it seems to be everywhere, and why not, right?

> ❝ 1. Hammers hate your thumbs.
> 2. Nails hate walls. ❞

So now you have your supplies. Good work. Are you sure they're the right ones?

They probably aren't. There's some amazing conspiracy in the crafting world that misleads you into buying every choice of glue just to realize you don't own the right kind for your project. It's like the eight-hot-dog-buns-with-ten-hot dogs situation. Things just never seem to match up correctly. So you'll probably need some space in your closet for unused glue, glitter, and crepe paper. There are ladies out there in Ohio who have ROOMS dedicated to crafting. ROOMS. Be thankful you only have a little closet with some extra glue and crepe paper, young person.

The good news is if you continue to craft, perhaps you'll use all your extra supplies. Probably not, but again, who knows? What is certain is that you have your supplies, you have your craft, and now all you need is to DO IT.

Doing it. *INSERT BIG SIGH HERE.*

Doing it is the real rub. Why? Because you have everything you need so nothing is holding you back.

Except for yourself. And I find the main reason that I drag my heels at this point in the craft is none other than Joselyn Hughes. Because I'm a procrastinator and there's nothing easier or more satisfying than blowing something off so I can get other, more useless things done. Like sending a thank you card to my dentist; thinking about Jonathan Taylor Thomas; calling my BFF Deb, who lives in Tampa; surfing Tumblr; surfing Twitter; pinning pins on Pinterest; and memorizing historical war speeches. The list goes on, because I continue to write it to avoid doing any actual work, you see?

So you've pushed past the self-imposed delay and now you're crafting! All right!

Crafting is such fun! Whee!

Until you realize you have no idea what a whipstitch is. *Screeeech!* (That's the sound of crafting coming to halt.)

Good news: the Internet is yet again here to save the day.

You know how much crafting 411 lives online? You'd think the people who enjoy crafting the most are too busy crocheting 7-foot scarves and spinning messy pottery wheels to touch the Internet, but then you'd be massively wrong. Crafters LOVE the Internet. There is a web page, video, blog post, tweet, podcast, Facebook group, and tutorial for ANY craft online. Look at me, for goodness sake! It's the only way I ever figure out any answers.

I fully support you logging on and searching for anything you have a question about.

So if you're looking at something in this book and think "Did I miss something?" "Joselyn, why didn't you explain this more?" "But how do I do this?" (Which you won't, because this book and I are both perfect, but IF for some reason that happens . . .), I implore you to Google.

I repeat: just Google it!

I will teach my kids how to walk, talk, yadda yadda yadda, but I will most definitely teach them how to Google. "I don't want to help you with your homework, kid! I hated math! Google 'algebra,' young Joselina." (Side note: I will be naming my kids after ME, so just like George Foreman, their names will all somehow be derived from mine. My kids' names will be Jose Lyn, Jos! Lynn!, Josielyn, Johnselyn, Josssss [pronounced like a hiss], JJLyn, and last but not least, Baby JosJos. Aw, Baby JosJos is the cutest li'l thing.)

So you pushed past distraction, destruction, and disillusionment, and now, drum roll please . . . YOU FUCKING DID IT! YOU COMPLETED THE CRAFT!

Sit down for a second, or have a shot of whiskey, or yell it off the rooftops, because what an accomplishment!!! Congratulations!

I am so fucking proud of you. Prouder of you than of my dog-son Jones when he graduated from puppy school. And he was wearing a tiny cap and gown, so trust me when I say that's hard to beat. But you *did it*. You're a winner. You're the best.

Gift

Can we take a moment to reflect upon life's gifts? A beautiful sunrise, the laugh of a child, a compliment of your backside. Anything can be considered a gift, depending on how you look at it. Take my mom, for example, who thinks bird poop is a gift of good luck. I'm pretty sure it's not, but good on her, you know?

Gifts can be epic and life altering, or gooey and come from a bird's butthole, but for most of us, they are a bit more tangible, usually in the form of thoughtful little trinkets designed to make someone feel special and cared for.

I love to give gifts. If you're wondering why, it's because I have a codependent personality, so other people's happiness takes precedence over my own. **Let's do the math . . .**

giving gifts = other people being happy = me being happy. **Not giving gifts = other people being normal = me being worried that they hate me and I'll probably die alone.**

I'm working on toning this down, but I personally think it's better to be slightly codependent than to be a total narcissist, because codependents at least give gifts, and have you ever received a present from a narcissist? Didn't think so.

So make some gifts for your friends. For your family. For your frenemies. For your narcimies. (Those are narcissists who are also enemies.) **I think, codependent or not, you'll find that putting a smile on someone else's face will put a smile on yours.**

These are bow-utiful.

Bow Tie Key Chain

What is with people who carry seven hundred keys, forty tiny supermarket loyalty cards, and a lanyard on their key ring like they're a goddamn prison guard or something? Seriously. There can't possibly be that many locks involved in your day-to-day. You simply wouldn't be able to function.

Well, this key chain isn't a metal detector nightmare. It's a classy addition to your *normal* amount of keys on your key chain and adds just the right amount of cute too.

Plus, I was able to make this correctly on the first try. Did you read that?! THE FIRST TRY. So that is awesome in itself.

Dreams can come true, guys. And it all starts with this key chain.

MATERIALS

- bow tie template (available at DIYDammit.com)
- scissors
- leather, faux leather, or other sturdy fabric
- key ring
- E6000 glue (this stuff is the best)

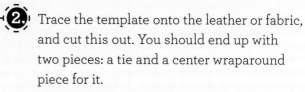

1. Print out the bow tie template, and cut it out.

2. Trace the template onto the leather or fabric, and cut this out. You should end up with two pieces: a tie and a center wraparound piece for it.

3. Center the key ring on one side of the bow tie piece and thread the flap through the key ring. (Don't forget the key ring—I may have done this a few times.)

4. Glue the outside flaps to the center of the bow tie using E6000 glue. (You may have to hold this to make sure it sticks. You can also use a clothespin to help hold it for you.) Let this dry.

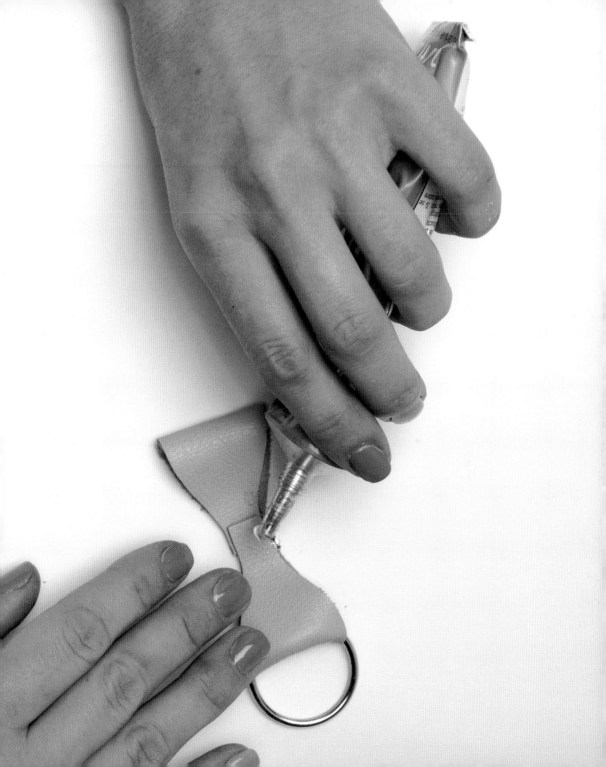

5. Take the center wraparound piece (from that same template) and glue this around the center of the bow tie to cover the glued-down flaps. Again, hold this closed for a bit.

6. After it dries, you're done! Go tie one on.

Tubular Frame

Difficulty rating: 🔨🔨

A wet-blanket friend of mine once told me that drinking from straws makes you gassy. This was at a diner where she asked for a separate check for her five-dollar meal and managed to frown while eating the most delicious cheese fries of all time. Haters gon' hate.

In honor of my decision to ditch this Debbie Downer once and for all, I decided to DIY with straws and pictures of smiling, cheerful friends just to spite her. And I farted happily the whole time.

I give you the Tubular Frame. It's totally tubular, and it's also a fun, inexpensive way to display photos of your real friends while also making a subtle reference to your ex-friends' faults.

95

MATERIALS

- 2 cute drinking straws
- X-ACTO knife
- photo (make sure it's a good one!)
- needle
- baker's twine
- tape or glue (optional)

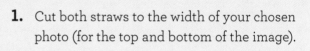

1. Cut both straws to the width of your chosen photo (for the top and bottom of the image).

2. Using the X-ACTO knife, carefully cut a slit down the length of each straw. (You will insert your photo into this.)

3. On one straw, using a needle, pierce the end of the straw and string a piece of baker's twine through it. Tie it off. Loop it over and do the same on the other end, tying this off too. (This will be used to hang your picture.)

4. Insert the top of your picture in the slit of that straw and repeat for the bottom straw.

5. If you need to, tape or glue the back of the photo to the straws to safely secure it.

You rule and other cards drool.

You're Welcome Card

I t's time someone spoke the truth about greeting cards.

Why does it cost five bucks to buy a piece of paper that says something you'd never say yourself? "To happy endings and new beginnings. Congratulations!" You just graduated traffic school. Happy endings have nothing to do with this.

All that being said, you have two options. You can spend forty-five minutes sorting through every card at CVS to find a message that is somewhat acceptable, or you can take some goddamn control of your life and make your own card.

Empower yourself. You're worth it. (**That** should be on a greeting card.)

MATERIALS

- template (optional—available at DIYDammit.com)

- chalk

- blank card

- sharp, sharp needle (dull ones aren't going to work)

- embroidery floss

- scissors

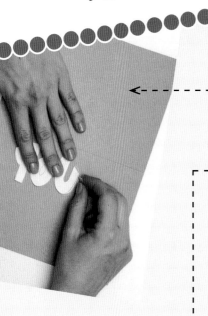

1. Cut out and trace the template with chalk onto your blank card. Or draw a design freehand.

2. Thread your sharp, sharp needle, and embroider your design using a backstitch. (The backstitch is a very simple, easy stitch. A quick Internet search will show you in no time.)

3. When you're done embroidering, tie off the end of the thread and tape it down on the inside of the card. (You can also cut out another piece of paper and glue this inside the card to hide the back of the embroidery— aka the ugly stuff.)

4. Go on with your bad greeting card self!

This isn't your grandmother's embroidery. And if it is, I wanna meet that badass!

Because I Said Sew

Difficulty rating:

Embroidery is cool because it's easy. There's something therapeutic about it. You can mess up whilst embroidering and not have it completely destroy everything. I used "whilst" because embroidery reminds me of olden times when they put e's on words like "shoppe" and "olde" and talked all funny, like "Penny for your thoughts" and "Please, sir, I want some more." Picture old ladies with those big-butt dresses sitting in a circle in a parlor embroidering things together. It's classic but cool.

There's a ton of embroidery stitches out there, but I'm keeping it simple because I'm stupid. And lazy. And a few other things. We'll do the fancy stuff another day. Right now, we're going to channel Granny and do some basic embroidery. Dress up in a big-butt dress if you want and get weird. It's really kind of a peaceful and pleasant experience.

MATERIALS

- iron
- fabric quarter (these quarters are a great way to get different fabrics without having to buy an excess amount)
- template (optional—available at DIYDammit.com)
- chalk
- embroidery hoop
- needle
- embroidery floss
- fabric scissors

1. Iron your fabric so it's free of wrinkles.

2. Cut out and trace the template with chalk onto your fabric. Or draw a design of your own freehand (much like the You're Welcome Card).

3. Secure your fabric in the embroidery hoop. It should be taut.

4. Embroider your design using a backstitch. This is much easier than you'd think (check the Internet for some great tutorials).

← - - - - - - - - - - - - ⑤ When you're done, tie off the embroidery floss and cut the excess fabric around the embroidery hoop.

Felt of Feels Ornament

Difficulty rating: 🔨🔨🔨

I have a thing for small things. A big thing for small things, if you will. These tiny reminders of whimsy are guaranteed day brighteners.

An ornament is, by definition, "a thing used to make something look more attractive but usually has no practical purpose." See also: a fountain at the mall, a bow on a bald baby, lipstick on a pig.

And if this li'l dude can make ANYTHING more attractive, that is valuable to all of us. When I'm having a bad hair day, I hang one of these puppies in the middle of my fro. I put 'em on the garbage cans in front of my building. I've even dangled one in front of a date's face while he talked about a skin flap and it didn't even feel like *that* bad of a date! Small things are the best.

MATERIALS

- template (optional—available at DIYDammit.com, or draw one of your own)
- scissors
- felt
- fabric glue
- needle
- thread
- stuffing material such as fiberfill

1. Print out or draw your template if you want to use one. Cut it out and trace the design onto the felt.

2. Cut out two identical pieces of felt (using your template as a guide if you have one). One will be the front of your ornament and the other the back.

3. Glue or sew any personal touches to the felt pieces (like the seeds of a strawberry, eyes for a dog, ornaments on a tree, etc.).

4. Place the two pieces of felt together (right sides out), and using a whipstitch, stitch around the edges, leaving about an inch open at the top (you can find a quick how-to on the Internet).

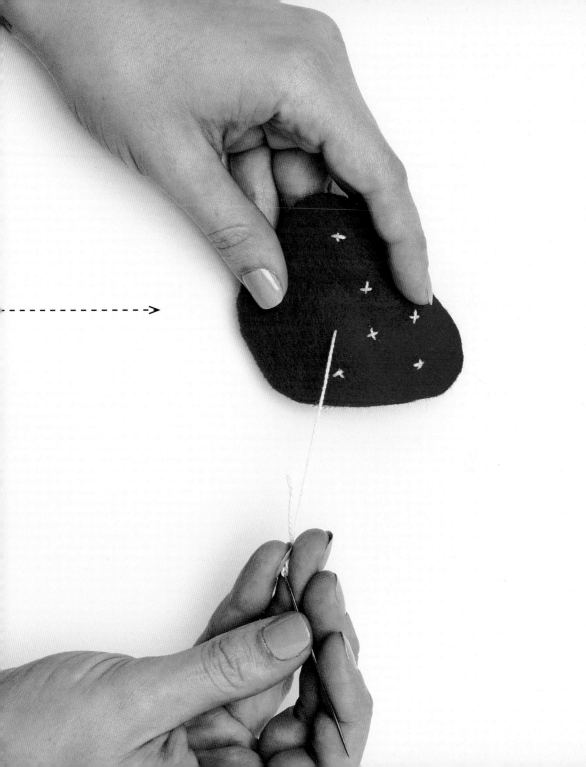

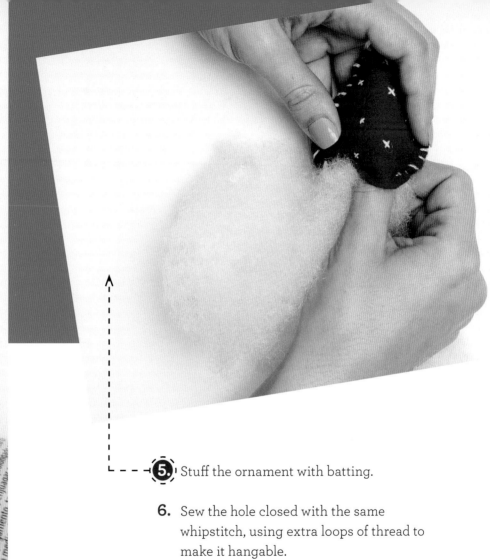

5. Stuff the ornament with batting.

6. Sew the hole closed with the same whipstitch, using extra loops of thread to make it hangable.

7. Add any other touches you'd like.

be
yourself!

Drink up!

Marked Mug (for Wine Drinking)

Difficulty rating: ⚒⚒

Mugs are great for not only hot beverages but other things too, like soup, cereal, or wine. Yeah, I said it. Wine. It's a hilarious joke at the office, but I don't work in an office. The question is, if you tell a joke while drinking alone in your kitchen, is it still funny? According to the wine, YES.

Now, wine comes in bottles, bags, boxes, and plastic, which means a few things: **1. It's not picky. 2. It's up for anything. 3. It's gonna love being in a mug.** Why? Because mugs are fun dates. Mugs are drinking apparatuses that hold your hand and say, "Let's experience this together; you're never alone when you've got me." You will never be able to express yourself with more gusto than when you're holding a personalized, wacky mug that says, "Cancel my subscription. I'm sick of your issues!"

Mugs are also an opportunity to look like you're drinking coffee while getting a pretty strong buzz. "Mug" rhymes with "chug." See where this went? Hide your drinking from everyone.

Let's make a mug. For DIY. For you. For them. For coffee. But really for wine.

MATERIALS

- mug
- oil-based paint markers (the others won't work—make sure they're oil based)

1. Wash and dry your mug.*

2. 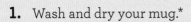 Using a design (available at DIYDammit.com, or you can come up with one of your own), decorate the outside of the mug with the paint markers.

3. Cook the finished mug in the oven for 20 minutes at 350°F.

4. Let it cool. Now, drink!

*I would recommend hand washing these instead of putting them in the dishwasher.

There's no one who *woodn't* want one of these.

Woodsy Ones Photo

How much wood would a woodchuck chuck if a woodchuck knew how to craft?

I have no idea, but riddle me this: Let's say that woodchuck had a smartphone and was on Instagram. What would his favorite filter be?

Again, don't look to me for answers, but I *can* tell you that people love transforming their photos into relics of yore (Earlybird Filter, we're looking at you). So why not try it in real life?

If a picture is worth a thousand words, a picture on weathered wood is therefore priceless.

Just like a woodchuck who owns a smartphone.

MATERIALS

- laser printout of a photo (has to be laser or it won't transfer)
- gel medium
- foam brush
- block or piece of wood with a flat surface
- credit card
- washcloth
- Mod Podge

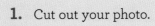

1. Cut out your photo.

2. Apply gel medium with the foam brush to the block or piece of wood.

3. Place the photo, printed side down, in the wet gel medium on the wood, using a credit card to smooth out any bubbles.

4. Let it dry for 24 hours.

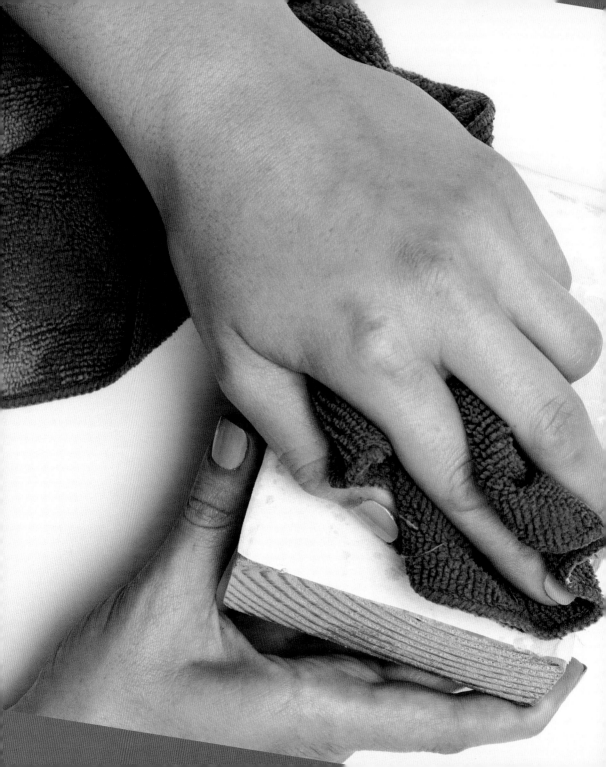

5. Wet a washcloth and gently (VERY GENTLY!!!) get the paper wet. As soon as it's wet, you can very gently rub off the paper, and the photo print will stay on the wood. (Be careful! If you rub too hard, the print will become damaged and/or hard to see.)

6. Let the image on the wood dry completely.

7. Coat the surface with Mod Podge and let it dry.

It's just lunch.

Looker Lunch Bag

Difficulty rating: ⚒⚒⚒⚒

I always brought my lunch to school, since the lunch ladies' food was stereotypically disgusting. Plus, I never wanted to be turned upside down by a bully so they could shake my lunch money out of my pockets. I also stereotype bullies. I refuse to apologize for it.

One time in the cafeteria, the lunch monitor had a heart attack. He ended up being fine, but it kind of changed my lunch-eating experience for life. I was just eating my PB&J and then *BLAM!* Down goes Mr. Rodney. It was weird.

This DIY bag is the second lunch-eating experience that changed my life. It's a looker AND a keeper. Literally. It's reusable, cute, durable, and easy to clean. Plus, easy to make, which I prioritize over anything else. So many great qualities!

I feel like I'm trying to set you up with this lunch bag on a date, because I am. A lunch date. Go on, now. It's just lunch.

MATERIALS

- measuring tape or ruler
- paper
- scissors
- ⅓ yard of oilcloth ("oilcloth" these days tends to be brighter patterns of vinyl-coated fabric that is waterproof . . . think tablecloth at an Italian restaurant)
- sewing pins
- sewing machine
- stick-on Velcro (isn't it the best?!) in squares

1. Cut a 15 × 12-inch template out of paper, cutting 2½-inch squares out of the bottom two corners on the narrow end. (If your template were a jigsaw puzzle, the two corner pieces on the bottom would be missing.)

2. Trace this template onto your oilcloth and cut out two identical pieces.

3. Fold ¼ inch of the colorful side onto the back along the 12-inch-long edge of each piece (at the ends that do not have their corners cut out), pin them, and sew across each one so the top of your bag will have a finished edge.

4. Pin the two pieces together, with both oiled/finished sides touching each other and with their finished edges lined up at the top. (I pinned them with the finished side out in the photos, but you'll want to do it the other way if you want it to end up looking like the picture on the next page!)

5. Sew down the two long outside edges of the pinned pieces (*not* sewing the corners closed). Then sew across the bottom edge.

6. Open up the bag so the bottom and the sides now meet flat against the table like a paper grocery bag. Pin the new bottom to the side edges and sew both seams. (It's easier than you think it is!)

7. Turn the bag right-side out. Fold over the top of your bag, and stick on the Velcro where you see fit to keep the bag securely closed.

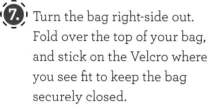

Coffee Coozie

Difficulty rating: 🔨🔨🔨🔨🔨

affeine, guys. Watch out for it. Caffeine is your best friend and worst enemy. It wakes you up, sure. But if you're not careful, it can rule your life. Then you're a slave to coffee and can't operate without it. You start saying things like:

"A yawn is a silent scream for coffee."

Or:

"Some days you make the coffee, some days the coffee makes you."

Or:

"Coffee: because Monday happens every week."

Don't be that person. Please don't be that person. Maintain some distance from coffee. Have a healthy, normal relationship with coffee. Don't let it carve your name into its stomach like Mark Wahlberg did to Reese Witherspoon in that weird stalker movie. Be your own person. Coffee only cares about itself. It's time for you to start caring about you.

So let's make this darling, reusable coffee cup coozie to protect your hand, your heart, and your emotions. And if you get sucked back into coffee's control, just slowly put the cup of coffee down and walk away. You can do this. I'm here for you.

MATERIALS

- coozie template (available at DIYDammit.com)
- scissors
- fabric
- cotton batting
- sewing pins
- hair elastic
- sewing machine
- needle
- thread
- button

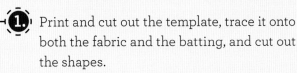

1. Print and cut out the template, trace it onto both the fabric and the batting, and cut out the shapes.

2. Pin the fabric and batting together, with the batting in between the two pieces of fabric. Pin the hair elastic in the middle of one end.

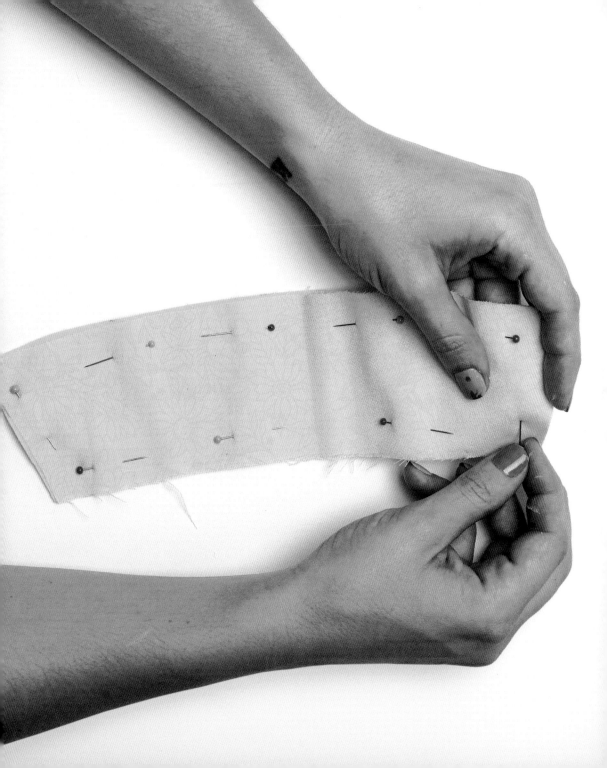

3. Sew along all the edges.

4. Sew a button onto the side without the elastic.

5. Place the coozie around a mug, cup, or whatever you drink from, and loop the elastic around the button.

Getting Inspired

Ah, beautiful inspiration. Maybe you find it in the sunset, in a rainbow, or during a long walk in a nearby park. I find it in dog farts. Mainly, because when my dogs fart, it smells so bad I am forced to physically get up and start moving. Moving makes me think. When I think, I realize inspiration is all around us. Isn't the world a beautiful place?

I digress.

When it comes to crafting, I am most inspired when I see something I could potentially make sitting on a shelf of a fancy store for eighteen times the cost of making it myself. Money is a great motivator. For me, at least. Although now I've gotten a bit cocky and with almost everything I see in a store, I think, "I could make that."

At other times, inspiration strikes, but you can't always craft at the drop of a hat, so I suggest writing down your ideas to inspire you later. I've kept a notebook next to my bed for ten years and never understood one thing I've written down in it. But at least I try to. **Does anyone know what a dream where my dogs are in charge and leading a brass band down the streets of Anchorage means?** Me neither.

If you're lacking inspiration, try looking at things differently. Shake it up. Try something new—a food item, an outfit, a way to say "Hi" to people.

139

> **Moving makes me think. When I think, I realize inspiration is all around us. Isn't the world a beautiful place?**

Turn upside down. Wear sunglasses or a wig and call yourself Tabitha. Play some fun music. Whatever it takes to disrupt your normal thinking.

Dig deep and explore some things that you find interesting.

Paying attention to details also helps. Maybe you take the same route to work every day. Tomorrow try noticing five things that you never noticed before, and keep doing it. **The more you notice the small details in life, the more they will inspire you.**

Taking a walk is another way to clear your head to make room for new ideas. Or take a march, a skip, or a jog. Whatever's clever, boo.

I've found that hanging out with kids and/or dogs opens up the ol' inspiration station. There's something about playing without worry or concern for anything else and being in the moment that is freeing. It's mind opening. Like when my dog Nugget chases his tail for five minutes. Brain. Blown.

You can also Google "how to be inspired." Remember, I am a proponent of the Internet. If you're stuck, do what it takes to get unstuck.

And whatever ends up inspiring you, let it.

Intermission: Mamrie's Guide to *Craft* Cocktails

Hey there, readers! Thought I would pop in for a sec and give Joselyn a chance to ice her hot glue burns. You might be thinking, who the fuck is this random woman taking over a couple pages in my new favorite book? First of all, watch your mouth. Second of all, I'm Joselyn's friend Mamrie! I am host and author of *You Deserve a Drink* and happen to know a little about a lot. But mostly about drinking.

Joselyn and I share an office, and for months I had to work next to piles of craft supplies while she created these masterpieces. **Have you ever had to shoot a drinking video next to a dangerously high pile of PVC and embroidery floss?** Needless to say, I almost drank Mod Podge on more than one occasion.

That being said, I am impressed with how handy and crafty Joselyn is. Or at least how hard she tries to be. Crafting is hard work. I see Joselyn hammering nails and it's exhausting to watch. I have a hard enough time getting hammered and nailed. Hey yo!

Which leads me to why I'm here. At this point in the book, you've probably been working or at least trying hard like Joselyn. **So I know exactly what you need: a drink.***

I might not know my way around a hardware store, but if you're ready for a little cocktail hour, you've come to the right place, my friend.

I know, I know. Don't look at me like that. Don't scream for Joselyn to come back. This is a book. She cannot hear you.

Fact, drinking isn't for everyone. But it is definitely for me! I especially love throwing one back while crafting. If you'd like to experience the nirvana that is crafting with a buzz, I've got news for you: pair the right craft with the right bevvy and you will have the best time of your life.

But did you know that there are certain types of drinks that work better for different crafts? It's true, and I am going to let you in on my wealth of knowledge with "Mamrie's Guide to *Craft* Cocktails." (Get it?)

- ->

*Drinking is only for adults over 21 who can drink responsibly. If you're underage, then it's definitely not fun. Skip this section immediately or I'm telling your parents.

Vodka

Vodka is great for crafting. Especially whenever you are working with fabrics. Cause if there's one thing I'm better at than the choreography to "Thriller" (seriously, don't test me), it's spilling things everywhere. I am the Sultan of Stains. Unfortunately, no one is impressed when you give them a Cutie Pie Pillow (page 35) covered in mystery brown marks. Luckily for us, vodka doesn't stain! In fact, it probably leaves your fabric cleaner than it was to begin with. True story, lots of dive bars use shitty well vodka to clean the bar. It's basically Russian Windex. Vodka is versatile! Vodka is delicious! Vodka for president!

Suggested Pairings:

Craft: Get Carried Away Tote (page 165)

Snack: Bloody Mary mix (technically a food)

Music: Michael Jackson, obvs

Rum

Rum. Arrrr you a pirate? Great. Pirates love crafting. That macaw on the captain's shoulder didn't just spontaneously grow that tiny three corner hat it wears; Hook had to make that shit. And with all those rough waters and hands on deck, he probably had a little rum to go with it. Crafting and rum go hand in hand. Just as much as crafting is a vacation from reality, rum is a vacation from other alcohols. Throw on that Hawaiian shirt and mai tai up some macramé, friend.

Suggested Pairings

Craft: Felt of Feels Ornament (page 111)

Snack: Plantain chips

Music: "Under the Sea" from *The Little Mermaid* soundtrack after you've had two of these

Whiskey

Whiskey goes best while working with wood, leather, and anything else you'd handcraft in the nineteenth century. Why? Because that's what I assume people were drinking when they were cutting down trees and skinning hides to make raw goods. In your case, it's okay that you didn't actually skin cattle but just drove ten minutes to a Michaels (after stopping for sushi).

No one needs to know that.

Just know that in my household we call whiskey "angry juice," so I personally wouldn't drink it unless the craft I am working on could withstand a couple throws against the wall.

Suggested Pairings

Craft: Timber! Doormat (page 57)

Snack: Dried meat . . . or vegan beef jerky, if you're like me

Music: Johnny Cash (as your hot neighbor walks by), then feel free to switch back to Taylor Swift

Gin

Well look at you, you little juniper minx. If you want to know the benefits of this drink in terms of stains, see the vodka entry. If you want to know the benefits in terms of crafting, read on. Being a gin drinker says to the world, *I am filthy rich, hear me spend money.* I'm impressed that you're getting your preppy self out of your mansion to make some things by hand. And your own hands at that! Perhaps you're taking some time out from investing your millions to craft like the little people do, or think that by adding some creativity in your life, your powerhouse law firm will somehow benefit. Well good for you. It will.

Suggested Pairings

Craft: Classy Clutch (page 155)

Snack: Caviar, natch

Music: Vampire Weekend or Paul Simon (either; you won't know the difference)

Tequila

Tequila is great for crafts that need to get done last minute. Let's say it's your sister's birthday tomorrow and you talked a big game about how you were going to make her a cute Tin You-Can-Do-It Candle like the one you saw in an adorable, and very useful, book (page 67). But then you got sucked into a marathon binge of *Real Housewives* and you've got nothing to show for yourself. Espresso? Get out of here you regal Italian man! Red Bull? Hit the road you nineteen-year-old extreme sports enthusiast! NO. You need to drink what any self-respecting crafter with a deadline would . . . tequila. Unlike other liquors, tequila is an upper. It'll wake your ass up lickety-split and you'll be pouring hot wax faster than that one scene in *Fifty Shades of Grey*. (I'm assuming. I did not read or see it.) Tequila can be great for any sort of craft, but I wouldn't recommend drinking it while using power tools. It's not worth losing a pinky.

Suggested Pairings

Craft: Puff Banner (page 51)

Snack: Chips and salsa

Music: "Tequila," aka the Pee-wee Herman dance song

> " You need to drink what any self-respecting crafter with a deadline would . . . tequila. "

Beer

Beer is the perfect beverage for when you've got a craft that is gonna take a hot minute. You can't be hitting the hard stuff if you're about to settle into a marathon of cross-stitching. Beer is slow and steady. It's the tortoise that *always* wins the race. The other added bonus of cerveza is, the more you drink, the more supplies you have for crafting. Cut the top off that PBR can and plant a succulent in it. Stick a light in it and make it a lamp. Fuck it. Tie a bunch of them to the back of a stranger's car and slap on a "Just Divorced" sign for shits and giggles. Who cares what you do? You've got a nice beer buzz going and live in a first-world country where people get stressed about trivial things like crafts.

Suggested Pairings

Craft: Leggy Headband (page 161)

Snack: Beer nuts

Music: The BBQ Radio channel on Pandora

Wine

Wine is great for everything. Don't let the people around you say any different. People in Europe drink vino at lunch and it's considered classy and progressive. So, anyone who tells you different is closed-minded and probably racist. It might make you a little tired, which is A-OK as long as you're not using sharp objects or machinery. It's especially okay after a long, hard day's work when you're unwinding with some crafts. You're just a modern human who needs to relax. Do it in style.

Suggested Pairings

Craft: Marked Mug (for Wine Drinking) (page 117)

Snack: Cheese, all of the cheese . . . or all of those fancy water crackers

Music: Jazz, baby

Champagne

Why the fuck is you craftin'? You fancy as hell. Can't you pay an army of out-of-work RISD grads to just make this shit for you? Ohhh, you enjoy it? Well if money ain't an option, drop the decorative tape, Scrooge McDuck, and immediately start gold leafing *everything*. Also, be a pal and loan me $20. Mama needs some more vodka.

Suggested Pairings

Craft: Tiny Finery Tray (page 225)

Snack: Strawberries

Music: Louis Prima

Good luck and cheers!
—Mamrie

Wear

Ugh, fashion. Who can keep up? Paying attention to ever-changing trends, purchasing those trends, and then wearing them without looking like a walking fashion "don't" in the back of *Us Weekly* is too difficult to do unless you're a model and it's your job to be fashionable. For the rest of us, our job is to be regular humans with regular budgets and regular taste who just might want to look cute sometimes when we're going out for beers.

But you know what's better than any hot, stylish accessory? Something you actually made with your own hands. Because self-sufficient badass-ery never goes out of style.

I'm not trying to cover you in doilies or some olive-green crocheted mess of a dress with one sleeve too long. I wouldn't do that to you. I'm here to prove that DIY apparel can be made—and worn—with pride.

Hell, even Lady Gaga wears DIY fashion. I mean, *someone's* making that shit. Pretty sure they aren't selling glittery foot-long lobster fascinators at Macy's. And if they are, Macy's will probably be out of business by the time this is in print. Because that, my friends, simply cannot be profitable.

So why not give some DIY fashion a try? C'mon.

See if you like it, and if you do, try some more.

God, I sound like a drug dealer. EXCEPT MY DRUG IS MOTIVATION.

Just be cool, bro, be cool. Try wearable DIY fashion and I promise you'll come back for more. And thaaaaaat's when I'll sell you the real drugs.

Practice what
you bleach.

Lighten Up Tank

Difficulty rating:

n the laundry world, bleach is my kryptonite. Mostly because it reeks.
Never had a good experience with it. Plus, why on earth would you use
something that burns your eyes?! Stay with me here:

Other things that burn your eyes	Reasons to stay away
Onions	Dey stink
The sun	To avoid blindness
Salt water	Those fish with the lights attached to their heads
Robots	Lasers
Computer and TV screens	You could use some vitamin D and social skills
Acidic stuff the dinosaur in *Jurassic Park* spits out	*Jurassic Park* isn't real

See what I mean? Bleach is nothing but trouble. But using bleach as a
crafting tool is straight-up HARDCORE, and worth the risk. You can vary
your design by how long you let the bleach dry, how you apply it, and where
you put it. (Just make sure you work in a ventilated area so it doesn't burn
your eyes out of your head.)

MATERIALS

- template (available at DIYDammit.com, or draw one of your own)
- freezer paper (you can find this in both grocery and craft stores; it's great for covering food to freeze but also for stenciling)
- scissors
- iron
- cotton tank top or T-shirt
- cardboard
- foam stencil or bristle brush
- bleach pen

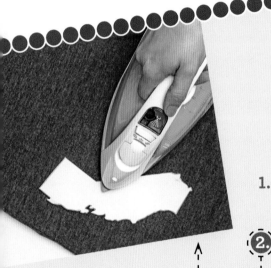

1. Print out your template and trace it onto freezer paper, then cut it out.

 2. Iron the freezer paper design onto your tank top or T-shirt. Let it cool.

3. Put a piece of cardboard inside your tank or tee (otherwise the bleach will bleed through and stain the back as well!)

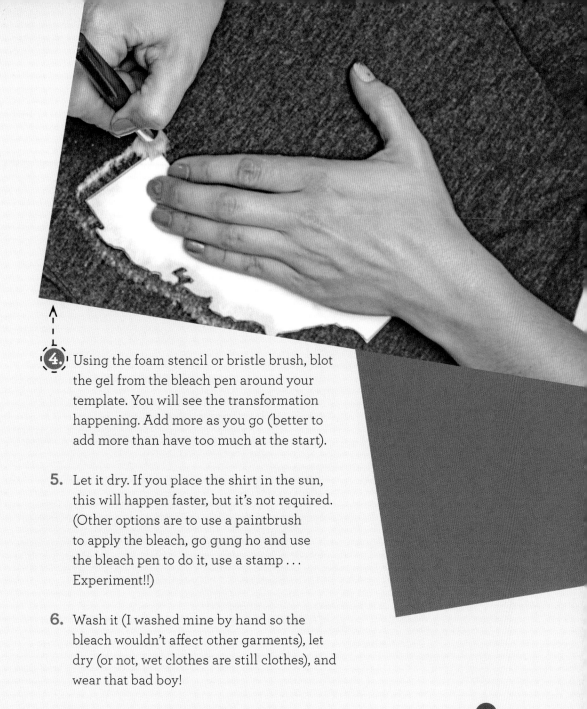

4. Using the foam stencil or bristle brush, blot the gel from the bleach pen around your template. You will see the transformation happening. Add more as you go (better to add more than have too much at the start).

5. Let it dry. If you place the shirt in the sun, this will happen faster, but it's not required. (Other options are to use a paintbrush to apply the bleach, go gung ho and use the bleach pen to do it, use a stamp . . . Experiment!!)

6. Wash it (I washed mine by hand so the bleach wouldn't affect other garments), let dry (or not, wet clothes are still clothes), and wear that bad boy!

Get to steppin' (out!)

Classy Clutch

Having a big purse can be a hassle. I have no idea how Santa Claus does it. In the dark, on an icy roof, digging through a giant magical bag of endless presents for, like, every kid in the world, and here I am in line at H&M, violently rooting through my oversize purse for my wallet but only coming up with eight lip balms, three old toothbrushes, my "safety" underpants, and every receipt I've had since 2003. No wallet in sight. Sooooooooo, because Santa is the only one who can work a giant bag, we're making our lives easier with this li'l clutch.

Sure, you can't stuff a lot in there, but isn't that freeing? Free yourself from the man, man. Plus, you're gonna love this li'l bundle so much, you'll probably make one for every outfit. And every one of your friends' outfits. And every one of those outfits' outfits. You'll be unstoppable!

Which I guess goes against the idea of having less. But less is more! Or more is less. This is America. MORE IS MORE.

MATERIALS

- clutch template (available at DIYDammit.com)

- scissors

- 16 × 10-inch piece of faux leather (or real leather—depends what's available/affordable/morally justifiable)

- fabric scissors

- leather punch tool or X-ACTO knife (the punch tool isn't completely necessary, but it will cut a cleaner hole in your fabric)

- button stud (these weren't easy to find, so I recommend getting them online)

- E6000 glue for extra reinforcement

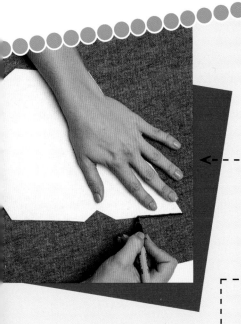

1. Print and cut out the template and trace onto your faux (or real) leather.

2. Cut out the template's shape in your faux (or real) leather with fabric scissors.

3. Using the punch tool, make holes in each of the flaps, or use an X-ACTO knife and make small Xs.

4. Fold one of the side flaps over toward the center of the clutch and slip its hole onto the button stud. Then fold over the other side flap, pushing it onto the stud too.

5. Fold up the bottom flap, and push it through the button stud, joining all three flaps.

6. Secure the stud with its top piece.

7. Glue along the edges of the bottom flap, securing it to the side flaps, so things will stay inside your clutch (unless you like to lose things; that's something different). Let it dry.

Go to page 176 to see
me wearing this cute
headband while cleaning
up un-cute dog barf.

Leggy Headband

Headbands are never NOT cute. Quick grammar lesson: that sentence contains a double negative, so we take away the "never" and "NOT" and are left with "Headbands are cute."

Headbands are cute?

You bet your patootie they are. Headbands make your head look like a present, and that, my friends, is adorable. Headbands say "Excuse me, WORLD. I am a gift to you. You're welcome."

So imagine taking your old leggings you stopped wearing or even the leggings you have on right now (I DO NOT JUDGE, NOR AM I THE FASHION POLICE) and using them for something else. Let alone recycling them to make a HEADBAND!? Aren't we not only a cute gift but an eco-friendly one too? I can barely stand how cute we are in these.

MATERIALS

- leggings (tights work too)
- cloth measuring tape
- fabric scissors
- sewing machine
- hair elastic (regular old hair tie; I always have one of these on my wrist if you need one)

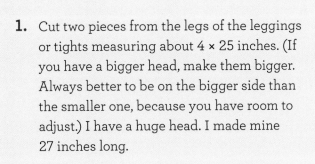

1. Cut two pieces from the legs of the leggings or tights measuring about 4 × 25 inches. (If you have a bigger head, make them bigger. Always better to be on the bigger side than the smaller one, because you have room to adjust.) I have a huge head. I made mine 27 inches long.

2. Fold each strip in half lengthwise and sew it together to form two long tubes. (For nice neat seams, sew each with the printed sides touching, then turn them inside out.)

3. Lay the tubes flat, making sure the seams are now in the center, and stack one tube on top of the other in an X formation, their seams facing each other. One will have the seam facing up; the other will have the seam facing down.

4. Now fold each tube in half so its ends meet, which will link the two tubes.

5. Insert a hair elastic in between the two ends of one of the tubes. (This is going to be your stretch in the headband.) Sew those ends together, locking in the elastic. Then place the other side of the elastic in between the two ends of the other tube and sew those ends together (see photo on page 160).

6. Cut off any excess fabric.

This is
TOTE-ally
worth it.
(I'll see
myself
out.)

oh
hai

Get Carried Away Tote

Difficulty rating:

Guys, I've lived in Chicago, New York, and Los Angeles. Those cities right there are the three majors, ya hear me? Three fashion-forward urban jungles that don't mess 'round. Particularly with totes. Totes are the lightweight bags that can carry anything, but mainly the message is that you've got places to go and people to see.

Whether you're transporting artisanal whiskey, unreleased vinyl, and locally crafted woodwork like the hippest kid on the block OR you're un-ironically carrying Dove chocolates, a VHS copy of *Bridget Jones's Diary*, and a wax-at-home kit so you can watch a movie and truly enjoy your Saturday evening like a boss, carry on. It'll be much easier with this tote.

MATERIALS

- tote template (available at DIYDammit.com)

- scissors or X-ACTO knife

- freezer paper (you can find this in both grocery and craft stores; it's great for stenciling)

- blank tote (available in craft stores and online)

- iron

- fabric paint

- foam stencil brush

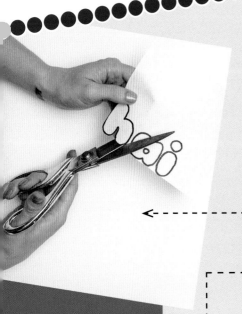

 1. Print out the template and trace it onto the freezer paper, then cut it out.

2. Iron the freezer paper design onto your blank tote. Let it cool.

3. Using fabric paint and a foam stencil brush, paint your design on the tote.

4. Let it dry.

5. Remove the freezer paper and you're ready to go!

You snooze, you don't lose.

Sandman Mask

Difficulty rating: ⚒⚒⚒⚒⚒

Ugh, sleep is hard. It's so good! But it's so hard. At least for me. Will I snore? Talk in my sleep? Drool? Yes, all of those things. But that's only if I can FALL asleep. Falling asleep is a difficult task for me. Until the sleep mask.

In general, masks are terrifying, but sleep masks help rich old ladies (who are terrifying) go to sleep. I might not be rich or old, but I do love shut-eye.

Without one, there are only a few other ways out there to get a good night's rest:

- Travel back in time to yesterday and go to sleep earlier.

- Stop drinking nine shots of espresso before bed.

- Count sheep—but only if you can count. Alternatively, you could also count the people you've slept with, though this could result in nightmares.

In any case, when you wear a sleep mask, you block out light and your brain starts producing sleep chemicals that help send you to Sleepytown. It also helps a bitchin' hangover, I might add.

MATERIALS

- sleep mask template (available at DIYDammit.com)
- scissors
- fabric chalk
- ¼ yard of fabric (softer is better)
- ¼ yard of cotton batting or felt
- fabric scissors
- elastic or ribbon
- sewing pins
- sewing machine or needle and thread—your choice
- fabric glue (optional)

1. Print and cut out the template, then trace it with fabric chalk onto both the fabric (twice) and the batting or felt layer (once). Cut out the two pieces of fabric and one piece of batting or felt.

2. Measure how much elastic or ribbon you'll need by using the actual elastic (or ribbon) to measure your head.

3. Stack the batting in between the two pieces of fabric. Pin the edges together, sandwiching the edges of elastic into each end of the mask.

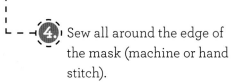 Sew all around the edge of the mask (machine or hand stitch).

5. If you like, you can glue on additional fabric around the seam for a more finished edge.

6. Get some ZZZ's.

DIY Disasters

What to Do When One Strikes

Whelp, you set out to make a candleholder and now, somehow, there's a five-foot hole in your hardwood floor, it appears to be raining inside, and your cat's missing. Typical.

DIY, Dammit! was almost called *DIY Disaster* because let's be honest: most DIY projects are just that. So when that crafting disaster strikes, first name it (I highly recommend DIY Disaster Sharon because it seems like Sharons are always kind of shitty), then accept it. Let's familiarize you with your additional catastrophe correction options.

Freak the fuck out. Ah, the freak-out. I'm really good at it. When things go south, it's very easy to freak. And it feels good! Here is my normal step-by-step freak-out process:

1. Experience something worth a freak-out (this can be a broken toaster, receiving too much junk mail, losing an eyelash, seeing an old person, and of course, anything associated with a craft).

2. Scream (five seconds).

3. Rip most of my hair out or attempt to (seventeen seconds).

4. Do fifteen jumping jacks (forty-three seconds, since I like to thoroughly enjoy each "jack").

5. Run in circles (ten seconds).

6. Tweet a one-liner about airlines (four minutes).

7. Laugh like I should be institutionalized (thirteen seconds).

8. Clap like they do at golf tournaments (ten minutes—I have a solid golf clap).

9. Take a nap (two hours).

10. Call my therapist (twenty-seven minutes).

11. Take another nap (eight hours).

12. Sing that 1-2-3-4-5-6-7-8-9-10-11-12 song from *Sesame Street* (two minutes and thirty-seven seconds).

Once I get it all out of my system, which only takes ten hours, forty-five minutes, and five seconds, I'm like a whole new person.

Google your problemo. I don't understand why people waste time asking humans for answers when the Internet can provide answers faster, more efficiently, and more accurately. I Google *everything,* all day long. Things I could probably use common sense to answer, I Google. Sometimes I don't even have a question; I just start a sentence and let the Google gods finish it. I trust Google more than any person I've ever met. Sad? Sure. But not stupid.

Run over it with your car. Go outside, place your disaster on the pavement, start your car, put it into reverse, and back over it. Then put your car into drive and run over it again. Then put your car into reverse and run over it again. Repeat this process until your stress subsides. So refreshing.

Spray paint the damn thing. Spray paint is your best friend. Like most drugs, it's a fast fix that does an epic job of covering up mistakes and making things seem peachy keen. Don't do drugs, but do use spray paint. But don't use it to graffiti. That's straight-up rude.

Buy it, for fuck's sake. Some things you just have to buy at the store. That's right, I said it. I mean, it's not 1840. We don't have to wake up with the sun to tend to the farm animals and harvest wheat. So sure, making soap is a possibility, but there's also the 99-cent store, Trader Joe's, Amazon.com.

I have limits to my crafting ability, and if I feel like something is too lofty, I buy the fucking thing. Don't be ashamed of yourself for this move. Tell everyone you made the thing if it makes you feel better. By not attempting to make something that's usually made by a machine (for good reason), the life you save may be your own.

More tips for disaster-prone people (me):

- Stay away from things that need masks, gloves, or safety goggles to operate.

- Buy the thing you want to make, copy it, and then return the original.

- Complete half of it and then call it "art."

- Only paint the side that shows.

- Buy an all-supplies-and-directions-included DIY craft kit from the Internet.

- Washi tape: it makes anything cute (notebooks, walls, phone cases, etc.).

- Etsy.com (that way it's technically still handmade).

- Call a handyman, preferably named Bill.

- Don't use primer, ever.

- And when all else fails, SUPERGLUE.

Crafting Mantras

Maybe you are sick and tired of being frustrated.

I understand. **That's why I came up with these crafting mantras that you can repeat to yourself when you're fraught with crafting stressors.** I find that repeating anything will calm me down. Especially when the repeated activity involves putting spoonfuls of ice cream into my mouth.

- It's only a big deal if I make it one.

- Can I get an "Om, Om"?

- Go slow.

- I can do anything I set my mind to do.

- Was that a dog fart?

- Work it out, girl.

- I wonder how many likes I got on that tweet.

- I got ninety-nine problems, but craftin' ain't one.

- I am a crafting champion.

Don't Mess with the Best, Cuz the Best Do Mess (It's Inevitable)

There's nothing like finishing a project and realizing you're surrounded by an absolute and total mess.

It's hard to stay clean and organized once you start crafting. Between letting things dry, making sure they don't fall apart, and making sure you don't set your house on fire, tidiness isn't a priority. It's actually a lot like cooking. **So I decided to take tips from a cook on how to keep your kitchen clean and apply them to crafting.**

Start with a clean kitchen. Yes, definitely. Clean kitchen is good. Especially if that area happens to be where you DIY.

Prep your ingredients ahead of time. Right, right. Okay, not so much ingredients as supplies. Get your supplies ready. If there are steps you can do ahead of time, that would probably help too. But who are we kidding, since as the number-one procrastinator in America, I'm not doing anything in advance.

Cook simple meals. Hmmm, okay. So maybe what they mean here is to not get too complex. Stay within what you know. Keep your project simple, without cooking it. Or perhaps they mean cook a simple meal to eat while you DIY. It all sounds about right.

Put away each ingredient right after you've used it. I like this one. But don't get confused and put your crafting supplies into your kitchen cabinets. Then you'll be glittering your chicken and salting your scrapbook, ya ding-dong. Sheesh.

Use fewer dishes and utensils. Definitely don't use a lot of dishes or utensils in your crafting. Fewer is better. Unless you are making dishes or utensils as your craft. In that case, disregard this rule.

Clean up the garbage as you go. I can get on board with this one. Don't turn into a bag lady, but do sweep up scraps and throw them away as you go. If you are comfortable around *any* amount of garbage, one day you could turn around and realize that Dr. Robin Zasio is on your doorstep, ready to shoot an episode of *Hoarders*. And while I do respect her kind-hearted, hands-on approach to therapy—as well as her healthy, well-maintained horse head of hair— it's best if you keep it clean, pal.

Clean up spills right away. Yeah, especially if those spills are glue. Or paint. Or glitter. Or anything, really. Keep on hand, close by, a bucket filled with cleaning supplies to catch those spills the second they happen. I call mine my Fuck It Bucket.

Enjoy your meal! Always. But don't eat your craft, 'kay?

Entertain

Having people over is stressful. **Not only do you have** to host them, you also have to TALK to them. Ugh, but about what?

Gas prices? Nail beds? Shrimp étouffée? BOR-ING! Luckily, this next group of projects is all about entertainment, and these are multitasking little suckers. **While they fuel the fun, they also provide some much-needed social lubricant.** Because you won't have to worry about making conversation when these babies start it on their own.

So when Dan the vegan is looking judgmentally at the cheese plate, you can show him how eco-friendly you are with your responsible cloth napkins. Or when that uptight Emily starts using words like "elucidate," you can drown her out with the absolute party machine that is a beer in a poncho. If all else fails, then throw this book

at their heads/in their general direction. **Not only will your guests be entertained by the book, you'll also find out whether or not they were paying attention to you anyway.** Two birds with one book. Just calm down. Have some food—and definitely lots of drink—and show off these cute little projects that prove you are the DIY host with the DIY most.

Pop-Top Poncho

Difficulty rating:

I love when inanimate objects wear things.

Enter this beer in a poncho. A BEER. IN A PONCHO. YES, I AM YELLING!

How can you turn down a beer wearing a poncho? YOU CAN'T. He's the party's VIP. The mascot of fun. The ambassador of "Hell yeah." And that's why your parties need these ponchos. They are a constant reminder that you can never take life too seriously, having fun is important, and beer is delicious. And once you start making your beers ponchos, you're not gonna want to stop, I promise you that much. But stop drinking. Seriously. You've got work in the morning.

MATERIALS

- poncho template (available at DIYDammit.com)
- scissors
- ⅓ yard of fabric (make sure it matches your beer of choice)
- fabric scissors
- iron
- sewing pins
- fringe trim (optional)
- sewing machine
- beer!

1. Print and cut out the template and trace it onto the fabric.

2. Cut out the fabric, including cutting out the two holes in the middle of the piece.

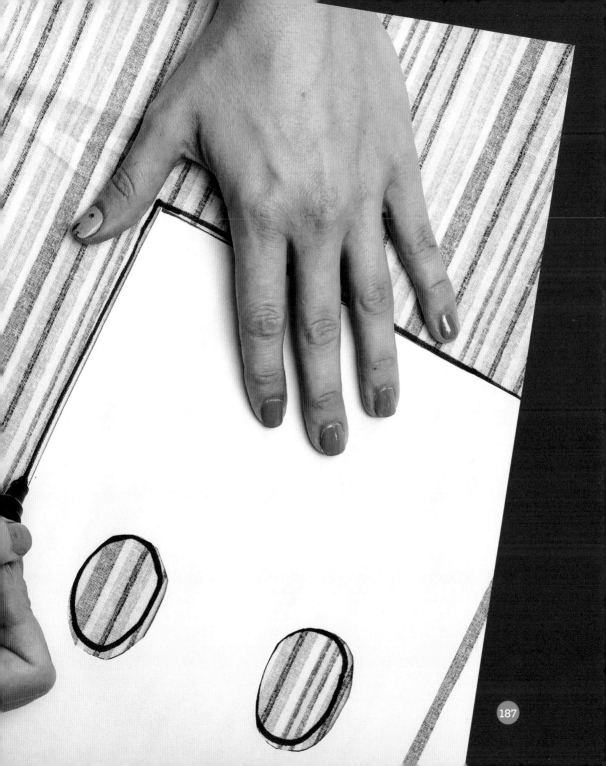

3. If you want to add the fringe trim, pin it along the bottom edge of fabric, and sew to the bottom.

4. Fold the poncho lengthwise so both holes overlap.

5. Pin the open long edge and sew shut.

6. Fold the poncho over your bottle of cerveza and fiesta with the best of 'em. Good yob!

Crafted Coaster

Difficulty rating:

oasters are designed to keep liquid off a table, yes? So you don't ruin said table, yes? Then please explain to me why on earth most coasters are made of hard surfaces that absorb nothing, stick to the bottom of your beverage, and end up dumping water all over you and your furniture. You don't get out of the shower and rub your body on tile, do you? No, you rub your body on a towel because it *absorbs moisture*. Unless your body is a life-size soft drink bottle and you were led to believe a large tile would be sufficient for drying you off. And even in that ridiculous, imaginary case it still doesn't make sense. Are you with me, guys?

I don't care. You can't have a nonfunctioning coaster. It's just not cool. Especially when coasters are so easy to make.

So I wanted to make some coasters for the beverages *and* for the people. Coasters that serve a purpose. Well, two purposes. Absorbing liquids and looking cute. Which we all aspire to do in life, no?

- 12 × 8-inch piece of ⅛-inch thick natural cork

- ruler

- scissors

- ¼ yard of felt (I would suggest using two colors, or two tones of one color, because I think they look cooler)

- hot glue gun with hot glue sticks

1. Measure and cut six 4 × 4-inch pieces of cork. (You can make as many as you'd like, but make sure you cut two pieces of 4 × 4-inch felt for every cork piece.)

2. Measure and cut twelve 4 × 4-inch pieces of felt (again, two for each piece of cork).

3. Cut each felt piece into four 1-inch strips.

4. Using the two colors or tones of felt, weave the 1-inch pieces into a checkerboard pattern, resulting in one woven felt square for each cork piece.

5. Carefully hot-glue a felt square to each cork piece.

6. Let the pieces cool.

Ready for
a super
fancy
feast.

Hand-Stamped Napkins

I gotta be honest with you guys. I use paper napkins like a monster. An environmentally irresponsible monster.

Because I never use just one paper napkin. I use *five hundred*. And I ball them up and shred them into dirty napkin dust before grabbing another, which is doomed to the same inevitable fate. It's a sad cycle, and I don't know what went so terribly wrong in my development to where one napkin led to two, which led to five, which led to five hundred, but I can't go back now. I'm in too deep.

Until I discovered that at one time, and even now in current times, people use cloth napkins. Cloth napkins! What an invention.

They don't turn into napkin dust, they don't crumple up into a small unusable napkin ball, and you can wash and reuse these things. REUSE?! Bah-bwhaat? Call Al Gore and get me a meeting. He should know about this.

And, as it turns out, and as someone who ruins almost everything she touches, I am easily able to make my own cloth napkins. So that means you *definitely* can.

MATERIALS

- stamps (tutorial below)
- fabric paint
- 1⅛ yards of prewashed fabric (preferably cotton or a twill blend—something you'd want to wipe your face with) or eight plain cloth napkins
- fabric scissors
- sewing machine
- fabric glue (optional)

How to Make Stamps!

You need
- craft foam
- small wood blocks (I'd suggest 1-inch by 1-inch size)
- wood glue

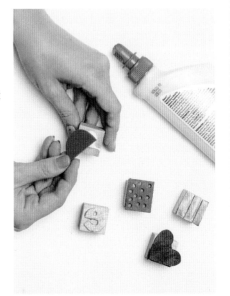

Cut out an interesting shape from the craft foam (check out DIYDammit.com for templates).

Glue the foam piece to the wood block.

Let it dry, then use!

1. Using your handmade stamps and fabric paint, stamp your fabric or preexisting napkins. Let it dry.

2. If you're using raw fabric, cut it into 19 × 19-inch squares.

3. Hem along all the sides at ¼ inch. (If you're feeling really lazy, you can glue down the edges with fabric glue!)

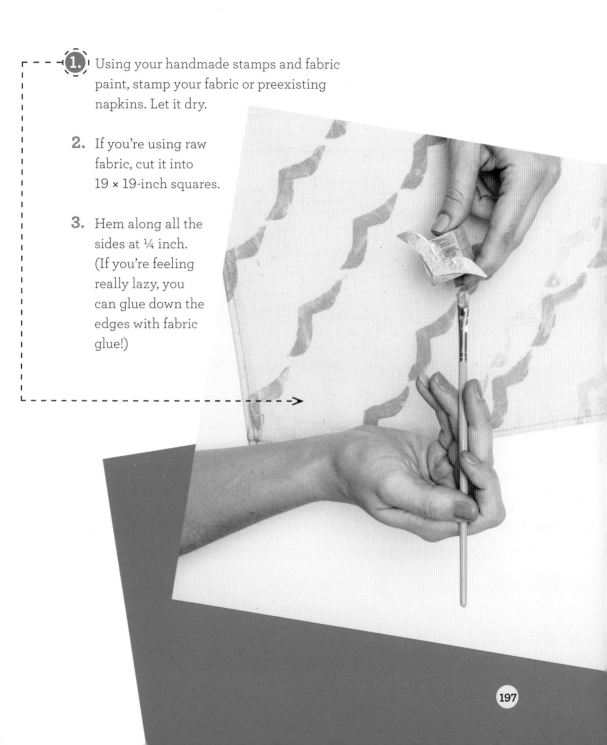

Platter with Panache

Everything looks great when it's chillin' on a tray. It's this weird regal butler thing, I guess. Partially because butlers always seem to be carrying trays but also because anything can seem more important if it's brought in on a tray.

Trays are essentially useless and usefully essential, which makes them MVPs in the DIY world, and really in life, for a hostess who serves cheap wine (in mugs) and stale chips. Tray chic.

Plus, I was able to make this without messing up one single time.

Jeeves, fetch me my craft supplies at once!

- letter stickers
- butcher's tray (this enameled tray can be found at craft supply stores, but any tray with a raised rim will do)
- paint pen
- glitter (optional)
- casting resin (not as scary as it looks)

1. Apply the letter stickers to your tray.

2. Outline each letter with a paint pen. (Paint or decorate your tray as you'd like. You do NOT have to do it like I did.) Sprinkle glitter over the tray too if you like.

3. Mix together your resin per the directions and pour it into the tray. (The directions will mention how to deal with bubbles that may form while pouring.)

4. Let the resin fully dry.

Notes:

- Most craft resins aren't safe for food, so make sure you don't eat straight off the tray's surface!

- Wash the decorated tray by hand.

S & P Shake-Up

I don't know why it's so hard to find cute salt and pepper shakers, but look no further. Because I made some. And you can too. Very easily, I might add. Go ahead and add a little spice to your life.

- 2 tiny jam jars (with lids)
- water-soluble pen
- hammer
- nail
- salt and pepper

Draw an S and a P on each of the teeny tiny jam jar lids with a water-soluble pen.

Using a hammer and nail, nail holes along the lines of the letters in each lid, enough so salt and pepper will come out when you're ready to use them.

Wash lids and dry.

Fill each respective jar with salt and peppers and get to eatin'!

Cute-as-a-Cupcake Garland

Difficulty rating:

This DIY can turn any location into an instant party.

Dentist's office? YES

Museum? YES

Car wash? YES

Broom closet? YES

Funeral? PROBABLY NOT APPROPRIATE (but yes)

And, if you promised you were going to bring cupcakes to your friend's birthday party but didn't have enough time to make them, this is a cute way of apologizing. Like "They're *kind of* cupcakes, see?" And then your friend will be like "Totes, OMG. That is the hands-down most adorable garland I've ever seen. I will only forgive you if you tell me where you purchased it!" And then you'll be like "Welllll, here's the thing. I MADE IT." And then your friend will be like "ZOMG WHA? This is actually YOUR party now." And that will definitely happen every time you bring one of these. So get making one!

MATERIALS

- mini cupcake liners (in the color[s] of your choice)
- baker's twine
- glue stick (remember those?!)
- scissors

1. Fold each cupcake liner in half.

2. Leaving a long free end of twine, lay the baker's twine between the folds of the first folded liner and glue the liner's sides together with the glue stick, sealing in the baker's twine.

3. Continue adding liners and gluing them together over the twine until you reach your desired length for the garland. Cut the twine, leaving yourself another long free end.

4. Hang the garland.

207

Make a
photo
booth
in your
house!

Mirror Fun

Mirror, mirror on the wall, stop making me look short and chubs when I clearly am so lean and tall.

But seriously, I feel like our relationship is not an equal give-and-take. I give you free fashion shows while trying on all of my outfits, anatomy lessons during my monthly breast exam, and every so often an advantageous angled shot of me making out with the cute guy I met at Taco Tuesday.

And what do you give back? Nothing. Nada. A blank stare.

So allow me to help you help me. We're going to take your basic bitchness and raise it up a notch with these fun stick-on props. They're quick, they're easy, and if I want to change up the design, I can get rid of them in a flash, which is more than I can say for the Taco Tuesday guy.

Aye, if this mirror could talk . . .

MATERIALS

- templates (available at DIYDammit.com, or draw some of your own)

- scissors

- black self-adhesive vinyl

- mirror of your choice

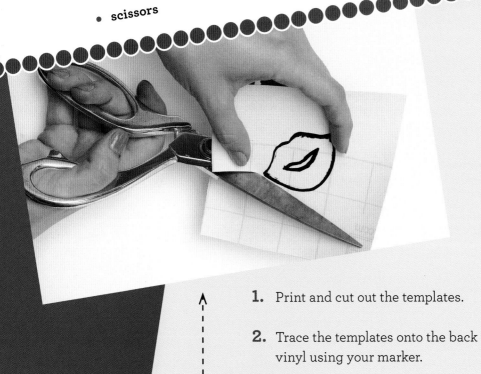

1. Print and cut out the templates.

2. Trace the templates onto the back of the vinyl using your marker.

3. Cut out the designs from the vinyl.

4. Apply the vinyl pieces to the mirror, and get crazy with it!

The Problem with Perfection

Let's look at DIY culture and its glaring, most obvious flaw. I never like it when cooking show hosts complete their prepping instructions, throw their dish into the oven, and have another nicer-looking, readily prepared dish in another oven that they pull out and sample. I understand that in the interest of time and, well, *interest* no one wants to show a dish simply cooking in an oven for forty minutes. But something is always off to me about it, and I wonder . . . Who actually cooked the dish? Does that oven even work? Does the food really taste that good? I call bullshit! **Just once I want them to spit out a mouthful of chicken provençale and rant about how fucking disgusting their recipe is.** Because that's how it works in the real world. Shit is rarely perfect.

When you watch DIY crafting shows on TV or click on a DIY post online, you aren't seeing that proverbial dish cooking in the oven. You're just seeing the final tasty product.

And *that* is misleading. Sure, sites like Pinterest are great, but with an overwhelming amount of

213

content, broken and deceptive links, sometimes very vague instructions, and unrealistic results, we're often led astray.

IT'S NOT FAIR. And that is why I created *DIY, Dammit!,* dammit. You're welcome.

Beautifully photographing a few steps out of a project and posting it online isn't giving anyone "directions." It's a show without the tell. And tell is very important when, as a non-Stepford wife normal human being person, you're actually attempting to make it.

I'm sick of all of us being tricked by catchy pictures and posts that make DIY look easy as pie. Easy as pie—that phrase right there is a lie in itself. Pie is an extremely delicate and complex pastry, folks! There's crust, then filling, then that lattice work for the top . . . get real.

Honesty Isn't Always the Best Policy

Ingredients for a "perfect" DIY tutorial photo post:

- professional lighting
- three months of preparation
- $thousands in supplies$
- all-day photo shoot
- patience of a saint
- seven assistants
- fancy cameras
- editors, editors, editors

Don't get me wrong. I very much respect the hard work that goes into making and posting these lovely pictures and videos. I just think they're missing the most important part: the blood (gross), sweat (fair), and tears (please don't cry over a sewing machine) it really takes to complete a project.

All Hail Queen Stewart

Speaking of respect, we must give praise where it's due and show some love for the pioneer of the modern DIY movement, Ms. Martha Helen Stewart. She paved the Oregon Trail of pom-poms and fabric glue across this fine country and right into our hearts.

She's funnier and smarter than we'll ever be, but crafts come first for Marth. **(That's what I like to call her: Marth. I'll clear it with her once we become DIYBFFs. I'm sure she's cool with it.)**

Marth is a bona fide hustler. A true crafty gangster. Before her, homies didn't even know anything about the crafting game. She done *taught* them, and here we are. A world full of DIY wannabes.

There was a clear turning point in the crafting world, a time BeforeMarth (though BM is a bit foul to use in reference to our holy Maker Mother) and a period I like to call the awakening, aka the AfterMarth.

The AfterMarth era has set a new standard for crafting possibilities, though Marth's standard may not be useful for most of us, because she is perfect. Like, TOO PERFECT. The rest of us aren't. **So while I love you, Marth, the times they are a-changin'. Who's comin' with me?!**

Thus, as we evolve from AfterMarth crafting and enter into the new age of DIY, Dammit, let's take a look back at our history, shall we?

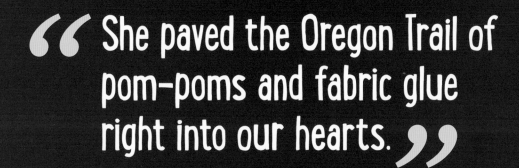

> " She paved the Oregon Trail of pom-poms and fabric glue right into our hearts. "

The DIYD Timeline of Crafting History

BeforeMarth:

1 million BM (or something)	Fire is invented.
15,000 BM	Needle and thread are invented.
1500 BM	Scissors are invented.
1400s	Scrapbooking becomes popular.
1790	First sewing machine is invented.
1830ish	Crafting ideas and instructions begin showing up in women's magazines.
1880ish	Crafting how-to books are published.
1934	Glitter is invented.
1940ish	Craft supply industry is created.
1941	Martha Stewart is born. (I'll let you have a minute to digest this major event in world history. You good? Okay, let's proceed.)

AfterMarth:

1960ish	Mod Podge is invented.
1964	Sharpie marker is invented.
1972	Martha Stewart launches a catering business.

1973	First Michaels store opens in Dallas, Texas.
1981	Joselyn Hughes is born.
1982	Martha Stewart publishes her first book, *Entertaining*.
1984	Joselyn Hughes makes her first handprint turkey.
2004	Martha Stewart begins five-month prison sentence.
2005	Etsy.com is created. Martha Stewart is released from prison.
2006	Joselyn Hughes sews her own Rainbow Brite costume for Halloween. Is still bragging about it.
2012	Joselyn Hughes struggles with an apple cider caramel recipe.
2013	*DIY, Dammit!* the web series is born. The game changes.
2014	*DIY, Dammit! Quickies* are born.
2015	*DIY, Dammit!* the book is born. Joselyn Hughes takes over the crafting world. The DIY, Dammit era begins.
2016	Martha Stewart asks Joselyn Hughes to be BFFs 4 EVA.

I look forward to a long, honest, and entertaining future as your new craft leader and would like to thank Marth for providing years of inspiration, creativity, and amazing photography. I cherish those times. 'Twas good while it lasted.

Organize

"**O**rganize" comes from the Greek word "organ," which means funky piano-type instrument that doubles as a donate-able body part, and "-ize," which comes from Tyra Banks's ill-conceived word "smize," which means smiling with your eyes.

That sentence makes about as much sense as my organizational skills. That's probably why I had to make up a definition for "organize." Couldn't find the damn dictionary.

Long story short, I try to be organized, but it's not easy. I'm a hot mess!

My keys, for example. You'd think I'd put them in the same place every time I walk in the door, as to make my exits more efficient, but no. My subconscious wants to have fun! So I sabotage myself by placing my keys where no one would ever find them: in the pantry next to my tri-color quinoa, on the bathroom shelf next to my spray-on leg tanner, in my dogs' toy basket, stuffed inside a faux squirrel that smells like dog breath.

Long story long, I used to say organization was overrated. But that's because I wasn't organized and needed an excuse for my messy behavior. I wasn't yet the mature and totally put-together person you see today.

As you get older, it becomes more important to learn organizational skills (and note to self: stop spelling it "skillz"). Organization is a very *adult* thing to master, you see. Just like you learn how to count, or recite the Pledge of Allegiance, or how the stock market works. I'm still behind on the stock market thing but consider myself pretty solid on the other stuff. Except counting and the Pledge of Allegiance of course. And organization.

Long story longer, organization is actually a great thing. You can breathe out a sigh of relief when you find things with ease. You can smize with satisfaction when you put stuff away like a goddamn grown-up. **Look at me—I organized my desk and now I'm writing a freaking book for God's sake.**

to do

m	MAKE SOMETHING!
t	Call Mom!
w	
r	GROOMERZ.
f	
s	Wine Yoga!
s	

etc

you got this, right?

Who's the Boss Board

According to my parents, when I was a toddler I liked to remind authority figures of who was in charge by whipping out my favorite phrase when I felt they seemed unsure: "I'm boss." So now we know who the coolest baby was. Moving on.

The more I think about it, the more I know how right I was. Because I am boss. I am one boss bitch.

When you're a boss bitch, a great way to keep your affairs in order is to organize them visually. And with this board, you can keep track of your to-dos, accomplish your goals, and handle your bizness all the time, all in one place. It's magnetic, painted with chalkboard paint, and ready to remind you who's in charge. Secret: it's still you. You also made it. You go, boss bitch.

Note: This is a 100 percent hardware store shopping trip.

MATERIALS

- ruler
- painter's tape (or washi tape, if you really want to go to that craft supply store too) and vinyl stickers
- 1 × 2-foot galvanized steel sheet (but size and design are up to you)
- chalkboard spray paint (real and awesome)

1. Using your ruler, tape, and stickers, tape off a design on one side of your steel sheet. It can be the days of the week, a monthly calendar, a to-do list—what is going to make you get things done?

2. Spray that side of the entire sheet with chalkboard spray paint, let it dry, then spray another coat. Let this dry.

3. Peel off your tape. (If there are mistakes, you can scrape them off and try again.)

4. You can prop this up on a desk or drill into a wall to hang it. (It's also magnetic, so don't forget to utilize this very important bonus!)

Fancy
metal
jewelry,
here I
come!

Tiny Finery Tray

I've never owned a piece of jewelry that was worth more than five bucks. You know that kind of jewelry—the kind that turns your skin different colors and screams "Sure, I'm cheap, but even broke people need to accessorize!"

The reason for this, my friends, is that I lose things. And I don't trust myself. And I'm not very wealthy.

Until this ring dish.

It didn't make me any wealthier, but it did create a tiny place for tiny things. Tiny things holding tinier things is about as cute as it gets. In a very practical way. Not to mention that this dazzlin' dish for diamonds and other assorted jewels serves as a great gift. I certainly can't afford to be giving out jewelry to my friends and loved ones, but I can afford to make one of these puppies.

I might even reward myself for this great DIY by purchasing something made with real metal! You should too. Treat yo'self!

MATERIALS

- craft paint and paintbrush
- 2-inch terra cotta or teacup saucer
- cute miniatures
- E6000 glue

1. Paint your saucer in the shade you like most. (You can also paint the inside one color and the outside another—up to you.) Let it dry.

2. Paint a miniature. (These in the photo are small birds and babies I found in the party section of a craft store, but check out HO-scale train set miniatures or other fun miniatures you can find online or in craft stores!) Let it dry.

3. Glue the miniature onto your saucer. This can serve as a ring holder or just a cute decoration on your jewelry dish.

Don't box us in.

Craft Outside the Box

I'm not a Carrie.

I'm not a Samantha, Miranda, or Charlotte either—what with their eight-hundred-dollar heels and designer handbags. I'm more of a Lena Dunham in that episode of *Girls* when she wakes up on the train in Coney Island at five A.M. without her purse. Except unlike Lena Dunham, I'm not on TV. I also didn't get three million dollars for this book. (But thanks for buying me Thai food, HarperOne!)

Needless to say, most of my shoes are affordable (cheap) and I have no need to display them or the boxes they came in. That is, if they even came in a box. So naturally, when I thought about covering and repurposing shoe boxes I was all "Ooooo!" and "Ahhhh!" and "Oh yeah, shoe boxes ARE ugly!" But not anymore.

Do you guys think Lena Dunham would like these? God, I hope so.

MATERIALS

- ruler
- shoe box
- scissors
- wrapping paper (preferably cute)
- foam brush
- Mod Podge
- credit card
- eyelet tool and eyelets (not necessary but it completes the look)
- button
- needle and thread
- elastic string

1. Using a ruler, measure across the bottom and both sides of your box, then cut out your paper to fit that size, allowing an extra few inches on each side. Cut out 90-degree angles at each corner at the same depth you've allotted as extra (each corner should now be missing a square). This will allow you to fold the paper over the rim of the box. Measure and cut out similarly a piece of paper for the box lid.

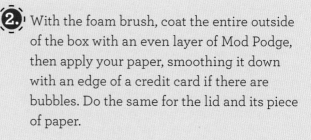

2. With the foam brush, coat the entire outside of the box with an even layer of Mod Podge, then apply your paper, smoothing it down with an edge of a credit card if there are bubbles. Do the same for the lid and its piece of paper.

3. Be sure to fold that extra few inches of paper over the rim of the box and lid and into the inside, even though you won't see this from the outside. It will give the edges a nicer finish. Glue this down too, and let the box and its lid dry.

4. Using an eyelet tool, punch and set two eyelets in the center of one edge of the lid.

5. Sew a button onto the center of one side of the bottom of the box, lining it up in between the two eyelets on the lid.

6. String the elastic through the two eyelets, measuring to make sure it loops around the button easily but still provides some resistance around it. Knot each end of the elastic off inside the box lid.

7. You can leave it uncoated or cover the paper with another thin coat of Mod Podge.

Customizable Calendar

I **am bad at time management. Very bad. So much so that every year** I forget to buy a calendar until it's too late. Like July late.

I am great at craft management, however. Cue this DIY.

Making your own calendar is powerful. I haven't started thinking I am God or anything, but I do realize time is what you make it. And what better time is there than crafting time?

Using some wood, paint, and rubber bands, you can make this perpetual calendar in no time. Well, in all the time, if you really think about it. But seriously, it's a pretty straightforward, easy-to-personalize project.

And much like the way you decide to spend your time, it's all up to you.

MATERIALS

- miter saw, or saw and miter box

- craft plywood

- fine sandpaper

- paintbrush

- paint

- stamps (see page 196 for how to make these yourself, or you can find them at craft and art supply stores)

- felt (I used felted wool; it's thicker than plain crafting felt)

- rubber bands (colored rubber bands are cuter)

1. Using a miter saw, or a saw and miter box (much harder IMO), cut the wood into pieces. Cut four 2 × 4¼-inch pieces, three 4 × 5½-inch pieces, and two 4 × 6¼-inch pieces.

2. Sand all the edges of the wood pieces.

3. Paint the wood pieces (customizable) and let them dry.

4. Stamp on the months, days of the week, and day numbers: On the four 2 × 4¼-inch pieces, stamp on each end and on each side of each piece a number, 0 through 9, plus do an extra number 1 and number 2 (it would be a shame if the 22nd of December came and you couldn't mark it!).

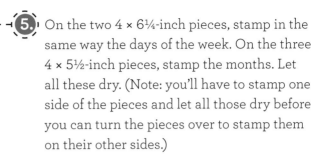

5. On the two 4 × 6¼-inch pieces, stamp in the same way the days of the week. On the three 4 × 5½-inch pieces, stamp the months. Let all these dry. (Note: you'll have to stamp one side of the pieces and let all those dry before you can turn the pieces over to stamp them on their other sides.)

6. Cut your felt to fit around the bottom of all the wood pieces when they're stacked together. (It helps keep them together and also adds a pop of color.) With colored rubber bands, secure it all in place.

PVCc'd Desk Organizer

Difficulty rating: ⚒⚒⚒⚒

What do plumbing and office supplies have in common? Don't answer that; it could be gross.

What do WE have in common? I'm not sure. You tell me. Write a carefully worded, two-page essay about what we might have in common, print it out, and mail it to the address below.* I'll get back to you.

Speaking of how similar we are, if you're anything like me, the surface of your desk is the junk drawer of your office. And your junk drawer is your candy drawer. And your filing cabinet is where you stash stolen office supplies.

But I don't work in an office, and you should stop stealing things. It's just not right.

Anyway, let's work smarter, not harder, and clean up that desktop with this DIY PVCc'd organizer. Because when you're already so busy trying to be productive, you don't have time to stop and put things away.

* The address is actually a fart noise. Sowwy!

241

MATERIALS

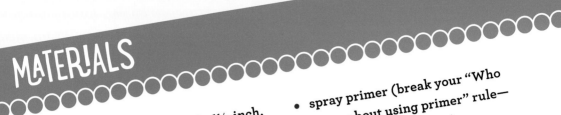

- one foot each of 1-inch, 1½-inch, and 2-inch PVC pipe

- miter saw (make sure you know how to use it and are safe!)

- coarse or medium sandpaper

- spray primer (break your "Who cares about using primer" rule—you need it for this one)

- spray paint

- E6000 glue

1. Cut your PVC pipes down to the appropriate lengths you desire: depending on what you're looking to store (pens, scissors, etc.), use what length and diameter of pipe will work best for that sort of item. One end should be cut straight across, at a perfect 90-degree angle, and the other end should be cut on a diagonal, at a 30-degree angle.

2. Sand the ends of the cut pipes to get rid of any plastic hangers-on.

3. Prime and then paint your newly cut pieces, letting them dry between coats.

4. Using E6000 glue, stick the dried PVC parts together in the shape of your dreams. The 30-degree-angle ends will be at the bottom of your organizer. This way, it can sit on your desk and the supplies will be pointing toward you.

5. Let it dry and get to work!

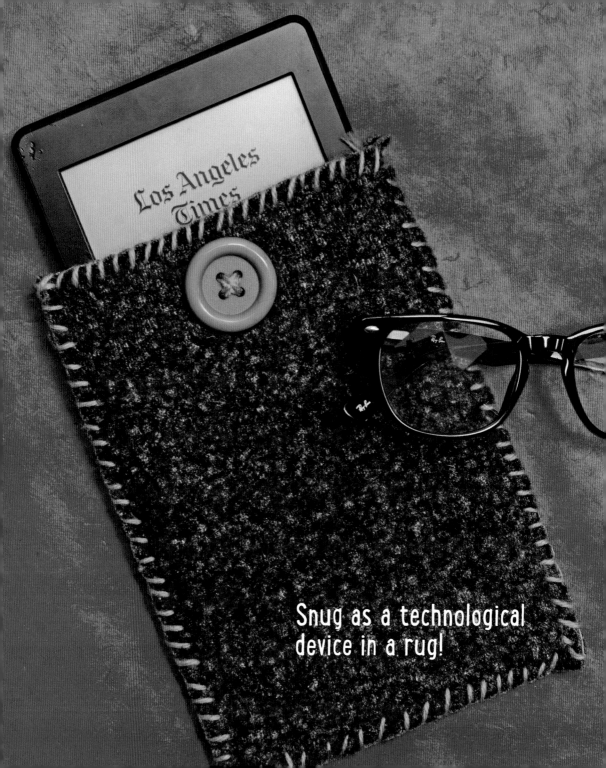

Snug as a technological device in a rug!

Tablet Tote

Difficulty rating:

Broken device screens are the most serious of modern-day tragedies. Sure, there are wars and starving children and sold-out Britney Spears concerts to grieve. But how are you going to play Words with Friends? Risk your finger getting torn to shreds from a cracked glass screen? I DON'T THINK SO.

AND I WAS ABOUT TO SPELL "ZAX" FOR, LIKE, 103 POINTS! LIFE IS NOT FAIR!

Sorry. I got all worked up. Which was unnecessary because there is an incredible solution to this worldwide epidemic. I present to you the Tablet Tote.

Bring the old and new together with this repurposed vintage-sweater tote. Your tablet will never be happier. The tote will treat your technology with respect, kindness, and most important, the same amount of love you do. Speaking of love, while you've got something old (sweater), something new (tablet), and something borrowed (this DIY), you might as well bring something blue into the mix and marry your tablet.

C'mon. We all know you sleep with it in your bed.

Mazel tov!

245

MATERIALS

- cloth measuring tape

- fabric scissors

- wool sweater (65 percent wool blend or more is recommended), prewashed in a hot washing cycle so it shrinks and becomes felted

- fusible interfacing (optional)

- iron (optional)

- sewing pins

- needle (choose the right size for your choice of yarn)

- yarn

- button

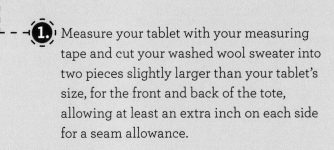

1. Measure your tablet with your measuring tape and cut your washed wool sweater into two pieces slightly larger than your tablet's size, for the front and back of the tote, allowing at least an extra inch on each side for a seam allowance.

2. If you're including it, cut out the same sizes of interfacing. (It will make the tote more durable and sturdy for a tablet, but it's not necessary.) Then iron an interfacing piece to each sweater piece.

3. Pin together the edges of your two sweater pieces (with the interfacing on the inside if you're using interfacing).

4. Using a whipstitch, sew along the side and bottom edges. (A whipstitch shows on the outside of the fabric and is very visible.) Then sew around the two top edges as a finishing touch, keeping that side of the tote open.

5. Sew on a button at the center front, then add a loop of yarn to the back that's long enough to loop over and around your button, securing your tablet safely inside.

What I've Learned (from Failing)

This is the part where I give you the best pep talk of your goddamn life. Why? Because if I can come far enough to write a book on crafting, I can write a chapter inside that book on encouraging others to do the best they can. Did you think I was going to say "You can write a book too"? Um, back up. Do I look like I want competition? Don't get any ideas, chief.

But you *can* accomplish what you set out to do. That doesn't mean you can pick up a bottle of Mod Podge for the first time and découpage your way into a successful Etsy boutique, but it's something to keep in mind on your DIY journey.

In any case, I think I've learned a fair amount about DIY crafting that is valuable enough to impart to you. I might not be a professor of crafts, but I am like the obnoxious kid who sits in the front and takes spectacular notes.

So here are some things I've learned:

First of all, it's your choice whether or not to label your attempts as failures. You may not have achieved exactly what you set out to do, but even trying is a win in my book. Literally. I say trying is a win, and this is my book. So there.

Second, remember to keep your eyes on your own paper. And craft. And craft paper if you're using it. Comparing yourself to others is human nature. But it's also very destructive. Some of us are naturals at a wide variety of skills. Some of us are naturals at being unnatural and awkward. Instead of wasting time comparing yourself to everyone, put your blinders on and don't worry about what other people are doing. Work on *your* stuff.

The key is to love yourself enough to give yourself credit for where you've been (Taco Bell), what you've accomplished (eating a Chalupa Supreme), and what you're potentially able to conquer (one to two more Chalupa Supremes). Which is everything if you've got your positive head on straight. (Okay, twist my arm already—*three* more Chalupa Supremes.)

Third, you rock and don't forget it.

Now go on, get. It's time to craft!

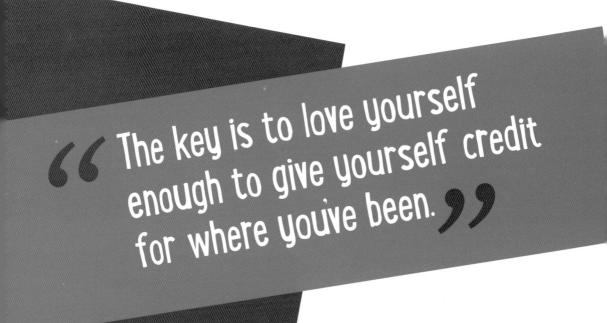

" The key is to love yourself enough to give yourself credit for where you've been. "

Resources

Did you make everything in this book, you wacky paint-covered, overall-wearing craft-smith? Whether you're looking to try making a project or just want to gawk at some incredible DIYers, here are some great sites to visit:

ABeautifulMess.com These girls have got it on lock. From recipes to décor to home DIYs, Elsie Larson and Emma Chapman provide awesome how-tos that are practical for your wallet, simple on the brain, and easy on the eyes.

AlmostMakesPerfect.com What's better than perfect? Molly acknowledging that messing up while DIYing happens. She gets it.

ApartmentTherapy.com This site has been a staple of my DIY cabinet since back in the day. Like the share-an-apartment-with-three-roommates-in-Brooklyn day. It's got solutions for all kinds of living situation–related problems, not to mention great DIYs and amazing before-and-after transformations.

DIYDammit.com Can you hear me over the sound of my tooting horn? Get at it!

FortheMakers.com For the Makers provides not only instruction, but curated DIY kits that help nudge you down your crafting path. Plus, they have step-by-step photographs to accompany each post. What a lifesaver!

Google.com I suggest googling "craft projects for 3 year olds" or "how to write a book about crafting" (super helpful to me these last couple of months).

HomeyOhMy.com Amy's blog is great for good-looking DIYs that don't take a lot of time and money. I feel fancy when I read her site—and who doesn't like to feel fancy?

ISpyDIY.com I love spying some DIY, especially when it comes from here. This is a great site to find fun, colorful crafts that are always cute. Highly recommended.

MarthaStewart.com Do I need to even explain this? Obviously, Martha has a team of people curating and crafting for her on the daily, but just because it's not one person doesn't mean it's not full of incredible ideas.

OhHappyDay.com Oh Happy Day is chock full of party-worthy DIYs that will leave you wondering how you ever threw a party without it. It's also full of other projects to do at home when you're a party of one.

ThanksIMadeItBlog.com Thanks, did you also make this site? Because it is rad. Thanks, I Made It has all kinds of fashion DIYs and even a few home projects, too. We're all welcome.

Crafters Be Shoppin'

Here's a quick list of my favorite craft supply destinations if you're looking for a little direction.

Amazon
www.amazon.com

Create for Less
www.createforless.com

JoAnn Fabrics
www.joann.com

Michaels
www.michaels.com

Plaid
www.plaidonline.com

Save On Crafts
www.save-on-crafts.com

Sunshine Crafts
www.sunshinecrafts.com

P.S.

Have you been pulled into the black hole that is Pinterest?

Do you keep aimlessly scrolling down, overwhelmed by the Crock-Pot recipes and salvaged wood décor? STOP. They've made it so you never reach the bottom—it literally goes on FOREVER. Lucky for you, I've waded through the panic attack–inducing amount of content for you, and found a few favorite pinners I can go to for inspiration without finding myself on the couch hours later with carpal tunnel and a diminished sense of self.

Vintage Revivals

Mandi pins everything and organizes like a champ. Her own site even has some of the best DIYs both sides of the Mississippi. Worth a follow.

Poppytalk

Over 100 boards?! You're damn straight. Poppytalk is another great resource on its own, but with the power of Pinterest, becomes an unstoppable source for DIY, décor, and entertaining inspiration.

Honestly, WTF

Honestly. This is a pinner's paradise. It's my cooler, more stylish evil sister's vision board in pin form. There's good-looking food, good-looking fashion, and good-looking crafts. And, again, another awesome DIY site on its own.

Acknowledgments

My mom and dad for being the best.

My family and friends for being the funniest, nicest, smartest, most wonderful people that support me and love me and I couldn't do anything without.

Grace for being my friend who wanted me to make videos.

Chris and everyone at Nerdist for letting me bring my idea to life.

Hilary, my amazing editor.

Elana Clark-Faler for her help and wisdom.

My reps for being cool af.

My dogs who have no idea what joy they bring into my life and will never know but I feel like I need to thank them and this is clearly for me but let me have it.

And to the superstar quarterback of the best team in the NFL, the Green Bay Packers: **Aaron Rodgers.** Everything I do, I do for you.

Share Your Did Its (or Dammits!)

f you've made a craft from one of these pages, from one of my videos online, or from a completely random corner of your amazing brain, good on ya! I like it! Go team!

But it doesn't count if you don't show everyone the good, the bad, and of course, the utterly adorable.

Share photos of your "Did its!" and "Dammits!" anywhere on social media using the hashtag **#DIYDammit** so all of us can pat ya on the back!

"Be Part of the #DIYDammit Community!"

259

The End